SHINE YOUR LOVE ON THE WORLD

Letters to My Daughters

6/6/23
DEAR
NANCY!
ENJOY
THE BOOK!
WITH LOVE
DR ADAM

DR. ADAM KLEINBERG

outskirtspress
DENVER, COLORADO

Praise for
Shine Your Love on the World...

"*Shine Your Love on the World* aims precisely to show just how exceptional a father's dedication and love for his daughters truly can be. Dr. Adam Kleinberg has provided not only his children--but all of us at any age--with a tremendous gift of timeless wisdom, beauty and love that is sure to leave a permanent mark on your soul."

--Jack Canfield, Co-author of *Chicken Soup for the Soul*® and *The Success Principles*™

"Dr. Kleinberg has clearly tapped into his soul's deepest love and purpose and can help us all learn to communicate more authentically and passionately. Brimming with a synergy of wise guidance from sages to scientists, *Shine Your Love on the World* is sure to motivate you while taking you on a truthful, poetic, and fearless journey into the center of the human heart."

--Dr. Jason Deitch, Co-author of *Discover Wellness, How Staying Healthy Can Make You Rich,* co-founder and CEO of Fan Page Generator LLC and featured in the documentary *The Shadow Effect*

"As a father of three girls myself, it gives me great pleasure to affirm Dr. Adam Kleinberg's delivery of a profound sentiment that dances in my heart. *Shine Your Love on the World* is a tender and masterful symphony of letters, poems and pictures that will open your heart and breathe childlike wonder into your spirit. Read it with your children, read it for yourself, read it out loud, read it, read it, read it!"

--Lee Holden, author of *7 Minutes of Magic* and PBS host of *Qi Gong Flow for Beginners*

"Filled with hope, wonder, and wisdom, this beautifully and passionately written book of letters will touch your heart, warm your spirit, and help guide your life's journey. Honestly and lovingly crafted, Dr. Adam Kleinberg's inspirational letters to his three cherished daughters about his hard earned, life's lessons have a universal appeal, and will be helpful to everyone who has an open heart. I really loved this magical book and recommend it most highly."

--David Jay Brown, coauthor of *Mavericks of the Mind,* and author of *Mavericks of Medicine and The Science of Psychedelics*

"Although it may seem like *Shine Your Love on the World* is written from a loving and dedicated father to his three beautiful daughters, Dr. Adam Kleinberg is actually sharing some amazing life wisdom with all of us. This book encourages us to get past our difficulties in understanding that life is but a vapor, and that we need to embrace life to its fullest. It also inspires us to let go of making excuses and to return to being the people God has created us to be; full of truth, passion and purpose."

--Dr. Edwin Cordero, President of the Sherman College of Chiropractic

"From the very first enchanting pages of *Shine Your Love on the World,* the deep love and connection that Dr. Adam Kleinberg conveys to his three angel-daughters is revelatory. This unique and insightful book will stir a hopeful enthusiasm within you and has stricken me with a feverish reminder to write to the people that are dearest to me in my own life. It reminds us all how crucial it is to express our love with defenseless hearts and to prove just how much we can really care for one another."

--Natalie Meadors, Lead Singer- Mojo Stone

"*Shine Your Love on the World* is an intimate and discerning work of love and devotion that touched my heart. I am impressed with Dr. Kleinberg's depth of knowledge in the broad field of human health and potential. I recommend it to anyone interested in a user's guide to living a better quality of life in the short time we are blessed to be on the planet."

--Dr. Liam Schübel, Author of *Cast to Be Chiropractors* and co-founder of Schubel Vision Seminars

The following words summarize Dr. Kleinberg's mission:

"*Shine Your Love on the World- Letters to My Daughters* is the first of a trilogy of books and my perennial gift to my children. I hope it will deeply touch their hearts, soothe their souls and become a treasure for them throughout their lives. I have confidence that as they become older and wiser women, they will refer back to it again and again for comfort, reassurance, love and hopefully some guidance. I hope you will, too.

Love and blessings to all our children
and also the one deep inside you!"

www.shineyourloveontheworld.com

Love ALL WAYS, Dr. Adam Kleinberg

Acknowledgments

I first want to thank my children Jana, Naia and Ananda for being such an amazing inspiration to me, and their mother for blessing me with three lovely daughters. Thanks to my dad Karl for his love and teaching me at a young age that my life was "all up to me." Thanks to my brother David for many years of laughter, friendship and unconditional love. Thanks to my cousin Lee for his love and being a great listener whenever I needed an ear. Thank you to my friend Anthony for his love and supporting me like a brother would. Thank you to my Aunt Joyce for introducing me to chiropractic and my Aunt Marilyn for continuing to share her artistry with the world and to both of them for decades of love and laughter. Thank you to my Uncle Barry who taught me to question the status quo and for making me laugh as hard as anyone ever has. Thank you to my grandparents Bernie, Leon (aka Chuckie), Norma and Jeane for all the lessons they taught me and the love they gave me. And thank you to my mother Judy for a never-ending belief in me and for giving me so many beautiful gifts through her love.

Thank you to my editor Nancy Marriott for her detailed and organizational dedication to make this book as eloquent and beautiful as possible. Thank you to Alana Demartini for taking the time to read my book and for her timely introduction. Thank you to my publicist Barbara Bishop for believing in my work and me.

Special thanks to Karen Tomlinson for her generosity, support, patience and for being my "first editor." Special thanks to Margaret Tudor for her loving and inspirational support and a very special thank you to my Bronx brothers and sisters who display a loyalty and pride like no other place in the world.

Finally, I would like to thank the Infinite Divine Energy of the

Universe for sending me unequivocal signs to follow my heart and to live a purpose filled life, for shining so much love and light on me and for continuing to guide me into finding an underlying perpetual state of gratitude. My heart tells me this is only the beginning.

Contents

Tribute

I see my soul in the depths of your eyes,
In the beating of your heart my love is true,
You are my blood, my tree of life,
I want to grow your deepest roots.

--Dad

(Picture placement inspired by the song "Sunshine in Their Eyes,"
verse 2 by Stevie Wonder. Google it!)

Dedication

Wonder Child

Everything I see is new,
The sky's a nicer shade of blue,
And look, the grass is greener too,
Since the first time I saw you.

Flowers grow around my door,
I've never seen that rose before,
And now that rose seems so much more,
Must be you it's growing for.

Cause you're a wonder child,
Living in a world that's all surprise,
You make me see things through your eyes,
Wonder child, its no wonder why I love you so.

Rainy days are bright for me,
Rainbows shine at night for me,
It's you, who taught me how to see,
Opened up the world for me, opened up the world for me.

Cause you're a wonder child,
Living in a world that's all surprise,
You make me see things through your eyes, through your eyes,
Wonder child, wonder child, wonder child
It's no wonder why I love you so.

Sung by Richie Havens on Sesame Street 1975
(Sesame Street Old School Volume 2)

Introduction:
A Bright Light in the Dark

Ananda, Naia and Jana
Central Park, N.Y.
July 2011

Keep me away from the wisdom which does not cry, the philosophy which does not laugh, and the greatness which does not bow before children.

—Khalil Gibran

October 2013

Dear Jana, Naia and Ananda,

Although I didn't realize it at the time, I started writing this book before any of you girls were born. Even now, for Jana at age 7, and the twins Naia and Ananda at 5, you are obviously still too young to read this book. But as I write, my words are intended for your future eyes, when the wisdom I share can truly touch your hearts, warm your spirits and help you girls find what you need in your lives.

The words that are now on these pages represent my humble hope to share with you—and with everyone who reads this book—some "wisdom of the ages" and the stories of how that wisdom came into my life. Within these pages are many of the great secrets of life I have experienced and my instructions for how to live in harmony with those secrets. The values that I have emphasized and want to impress upon you the most are those of *inspiration, love, health, success, happiness and freedom.*

The road of life can be a bumpy one. It is all too easy to veer off course. Without methods and philosophies that you have learned to trust, it can be hard to get back on the road to where you want to go. Sometimes it can take a long time to find what you need in order to move forward. For many people, life simply passes them by without them ever finding their way back to their path at all. That is not the life I envision for you girls.

All three of you inspired this book. I wrote it because I wanted you to know how I came about my life's greatest discoveries. I wanted you to understand what I had to rise above in order to become and stay healthy, and what I had to learn in order to liberate myself from my childhood indoctrinations. I wanted you to know the person that I aspire to be and also what I aspire to do with my precious life.

This book is dedicated to you, but it is truly for everyone—all fathers and mothers, daughters and sons. I hope it will help those who read it to find their own voice in expressing themselves to those they love, and also to help them to aspire to their own higher ideals in their lives.

By reading about my development—my "mistakes" and my unique path—I hope that you (and other readers) will be able to see your own path more clearly. I have faith that by sharing my own experience you girls will be better able to envision your own potential futures, and you can choose the most positive and necessary actions for your future's fulfillment. These secrets I'm sharing for achieving a deeper state of love, a greater state of health and well-being, greater empowerment and self-determination, happiness, gratitude and freedom need to be shared with the world. Thank you for inspiring me to do that through writing to you, my three daughters.

I have wanted to write for many years. I have outlined many books, written many passages, but none of them ever felt authentic. Nothing I wrote could ever have been as important or as candid as this book has turned out to be. You three girls were the catalyst I needed to finally "shine my love on the world" through this book. My hope is that this book may be a catalyst for you and for others to shine your love in whatever ways are meaningful to you.

I have a recurring vision of one of you, as a young woman, reading this book in the future. (The vision actually represents all three of you and could also be seen to represent all of humanity.) You are reading it outside on a beautiful sunny day, and, as you read, a passage deeply touches your heart. Your realization causes laughter and tears at the same time, and you feel gratitude that your father took the time to write this book to you and to the world, that he valued his beliefs and philosophies with such passion and dedication, and that he wanted to record and share them with you and with everyone in this way.

In my vision, you are looking up to the sky, thanking me and feeling my presence. As you take a deep breath and close your eyes, a warm wave of love and deep peace fills your body and mind. I promise that when you thank me, I will find a way, even from the great beyond if need be, to let you know you are so very welcome. Know that the word "quit" does not exist for me, and I will always be with you!

As I have needed to do, you too, my daughters, will need to find your way on your journey down life's bumpy road. Let this book be a bright light in the dark to get you back on the road whenever you may need it. In my heart, the great hope I have for this book is that in some small or perhaps profound ways it leads not only the three of you but also a multitude of people down that less traveled road and onto the path in life you truly want to follow.

All my love,
Dad

Part I
Inspiration

Ananda and Naia
Burlingame, Calif.
April 2008

Kris Carlson and the Stockton Bridge Grill

Naia and Ananda
Robert Moses State Park, Long Island, N.Y.
August 2012

My father gave me the greatest gift anyone can give another person, he believed in me.

—Jim Valvano

September 2010

Dear girls,

While we were all still living in Santa Cruz, California, I was introduced to a woman named Kris Carlson at the Stockton Bridge Grill, a local restaurant in the neighboring town of Capitola.

Capitola is a picturesque little coastal town with pastel houses garnishing the hills that rise up and away from the Pacific Ocean. Lee, the owner of the restaurant, has two children who were in their late teens at the time. He and I would often reminisce about the trials and tribulations of fatherhood, and he always had great advice for me. He and his girlfriend Jill introduced me to Kris quite casually one night at the restaurant.

Kris was the wife of best-selling author Richard Carlson and an author in her own right. Richard Carlson authored 20 books, including his 12th and most successful book, *Don't Sweat the Small Stuff...and It's All Small Stuff*. After expressing my affinity for her husband's work and my interest in meeting him, she informed me that Richard had passed away in 2006 on a flight to New York on his way to promote his latest book. Apparently he died from a pulmonary embolism. He was father to two teenage daughters and was 45 years old when he passed, just three years older than I am now.

I was saddened and shocked. The news got me to thinking about the "what ifs?" of life, and I wondered: What if something happened to me while you three girls are still so young? How would you ever know me? How would I be able to pass my life's lessons along to you? What would you have from me to always remember how much I love you and what I value? All the wisdom I have gathered and hope to share with you would pass away with me.

This "chance" encounter with Kris Carlson was the main inspiration for me to create this book you now hold in your hands. Perhaps there are some pearls of wisdom you will take along with you from these letters. In my mind's eye, I can see you many years from now telling your own daughters and granddaughters stories about this book and the future books your daddy wrote for you and the karma of our lives.

Understand that you girls created this book. It is your purity and beauty that has stirred a passion in me like nothing in my life ever before. I have labored to not overlook a single detail. You have been the muses to my divine inspiration. You bring out the very best in me. Please know that my goals as your father are to invigorate your passion, to sharpen and strengthen your minds and bodies, and to open your heart to a spiritual path, one that values virtues such as freedom, justice, beauty, truth, gratitude, peace, joy and loving kindness.

I believe that children choose their parents and that parents choose their children. We are each other's teachers. In the Buddhist traditions, it is said that if you even rub elbows in passing with someone, then you have known each other for a thousand lifetimes. The greatest gift of my life is being your father. How wonderful and amazing it is that we have found each other again!

Love always,
Dad

A Vacation Longer Than Expected

Naia, Jana and Ananda
Bronx Botanical Gardens
July 2011

You can hug me every day in your heart.

— Jana Aum Kleinberg
(At 5 years old, and in response to my statement
"I wish I could hug you every day.")

April 2011

Dear girls,

One year ago, your mother took the three of you on a vacation to Smiths Falls in Ontario, Canada, to spend a little time with her parents and family. We had relocated to Santa Monica from Santa Cruz just six weeks prior to your departure, and your mother and I had been going through a tough time. I had undoubtedly moved us around a lot and was having trouble finding a permanent home for us that would suit all our needs.

For some time, you girls had been attracting a lot of interest from casting agents in the movie industry, which is why I chose to move us to the Los Angeles area. It had gotten so that your mother and I could not walk anywhere without being stopped by people complimenting the three of you and, more than occasionally, expressing interest in you professionally. After we arrived in Los Angeles, a sweet photographer fell in love with all three of you and offered to do a free photo shoot of our family on the beach. A few of the photos taken that day are in this book.

Having three children in less than two years can certainly put a big strain on a couple, even in the best of marriages. The other details of why your mother and I parted ways were handled by us agreeing to disagree, but when your mother told me she was not going to return with you girls from Canada, that was very different.

I found myself alone in a three-bedroom townhouse surrounded by all the things that reminded me of you. My world had fallen out from under me, and I was devastated. I was okay with your mother deciding she'd endured enough of our relationship, but I was *not* okay with being separated from my daughters and you girls being separated from your father. I had every intention of playing the largest role in your lives that I could, and no one could question my love and dedication to every detail of your well-being.

It was an emotionally hard time for me. All of a sudden, I couldn't kiss or hug my three girls when I wanted to. As a chiropractor, I couldn't be there to adjust your spines to help with a fever or cough in the middle of the night. I couldn't tip toe into your rooms to watch you sleep. I couldn't hear your laughter. I didn't even know the next time I would see any of you. Jana's fourth birthday was an emotionally challenging day for me and is the only one of your birthdays I have not been able to celebrate with the three of you.

I admit I could have treated your mother better. She often bore the brunt of my aggression toward the world. I was angry and frustrated that things had not been going my way for several years. Several opportunities for my chiropractic practice to become established had gone poorly, and the experience had left me psychologically exhausted. I had also discovered a lot about the way the world works behind the scenes, the unscrupulous ways in which people are manipulated by systems they trust, which hardened me to some degree. In spite of this, I hope you understand that your mother and I had been the best of friends.

Not long before you all left for Canada, your mother had told me tenderly that the last thing she hoped to see before she died was my face. I was touched. We had shared so much in such a short amount of time. I wrote her poetry and read entire books aloud to her. We had a very deep spiritual connection and often cried and laughed together.

Your mother had her reasons for deciding to stay in Canada with the three of you, and I don't think we will ever agree on the details of her decision. Regardless of what had unfolded in our relationship, she did not have the legal right to make the exclusive decision to separate you girls from your father. Even so, I was confused about what to do. Against much advice from family and friends, I chose not to file felony-kidnapping charges against your mother with the Los Angeles district attorney. I did not think it wise for her to be a wanted felon in the U.S., unable to return without facing arrest.

Instead, I chose to pursue your return through the California courts and filed a Hague Petition for International Child Abduction with the Department of State. The outcome of my efforts would be one that baffled me as well as all the lawyers that I consulted. A series of unfortunately timed events and complications of bureaucracy led to your mother somehow being able to keep you in Canada.

The court proceedings were truly a charade of justice. Judge B. Scott Silverman is a name I will always associate with incompetence, apathy, even idiocy. The simple truth is he did not follow the law in our case. After 15 months of intense California court battles and me exhausting all my resources and that of my parents and dear friends, I eventually chose to mediate in the Canadian courts with your mother. As usual, only the lawyers made out well through this tedious drawn out process.

In addition to my failed California court struggles, I got to spend a cold, self-reflective, night in jail after a surprise visit and resulting altercation with your mother. A young inmate in the same holding cell lent me his jacket. Thank heavens that the ridiculous charges of assault and child endangerment were later dropped.

But that night in jail should have been a night I spent with Jana at the San Francisco Ballet. You girls were visiting me while I was living in Burlingame, California just south of the city, and I had tickets for Jana and me to see *Coppelia*, a comic ballet that had first been performed by the Paris Opera Ballet in 1870. Jana was in her best dress and ready to go when there was a loud knock at the door—the surprise visit that resulted in me being arrested in my own home without being asked even one question about our situation. Later that night, in the holding cell, I realized from observing the other inmates just how abundant and rewarding my life had been. Those young people in that jail had never had a chance in life, and I doubted they'd been given any of the opportunities my blessed life has afforded me.

The why-it-all-happened-this-way of the situation, while important, is not what primarily concerns me. What does concern me is that you three girls and I were separated from each other against our will. Our separation was against my will because I had always intended to raise you with as much love, daily guidance and affection as possible. It was against your will because you were too young, and still are too young to be able to express your own voice. However, even though I would prefer to be in your lives every day, I have chosen to accept our karma and make the best of it. (Some of this explanation may prove difficult to read and absorb, but I prefer that you have the story on paper, just the way I want to express it to you. Someday, I may no longer have the opportunity to do so.)

Your mother has read this letter and, although there are parts she may feel differently about, she is allowing me to freely express my own views. I give her a lot of credit for that. The truth is never absolute. Your mother will have her side of the story, and she will have valid points, too.

But regardless of differences, one parent cannot legally take the couple's children and permanently leave the country without the permission of the other parent. All the lawyers and the Department of State explained this to me as a fact of law, yet our dismal judge chose to ignore it. When I look back on the situation, I am still baffled by the series of events that took place. But the end result was the judge pronounced a temporary order allowing you to remain in Canada, which in turn nullified my Hague Petition.

I am sincerely not trying to vilify your mother. She did what she felt she needed to do. Your mom loves you just as much as I do, and she is a great mother. Our philosophy of life is similar enough that I don't have to worry about how she is raising each one of you. I am also infinitely grateful to her for bringing all three of you into the world. You girls have been the greatest thrill and the most wonderful gifts in my life.

Your mother has also unintentionally given me the gift of an opportunity to become more emotionally disciplined. Loss and suffering can very well lead to emotional and spiritual growth in life. Also, know that your mother and I deeply loved each other. We went through a tremendous growth phase of our lives while we were together. We made you out of love, and we will always have the connection of you girls. So, although it may be hard to believe, in my heart I will always have eternal love and gratitude for her.

Part of my growth from this ordeal was having my eyes opened to the incompetent and absurdly bureaucratic justice system we have in the United States. The treatment of fathers in family court cases should be more accurately described as *guilty until proven innocent*, and not the other way around. Fathers in family court disputes are treated as second-rate parents. I did not have an ounce of faith in the justice system before all this began, and why I thought it would be different for me, I don't exactly know. I guess everyone tries to stay positive about their circumstances, but it seems to me that justice is rarely served, especially for us fathers.

The bottom line is that each person's unique situation is just one tiny grain of sand on a beach made up of millions of grains of sand. Unfortunately, we are treated like cattle by strangers who are designated to make intimate decisions from within a corrupt system full of apathy and greed. I watched Judge Silverman nearly fall asleep while on the bench listening to cases prior to ours.

I now spend about three months a year with the three of you. I remain hopeful that there will come a day when you may choose to return to live with me of your own free will. But whether I am living with you or without you, I will remain dedicated to you as the best possible father I can be.

When you spend the time with me I have been allotted, I promise to show you as much of life as possible. I will take you to the ballet, the symphony, the Monterey Jazz festival, the U.S. Open, the surfing competition called Mavericks. I will take you to meet Amma the hugging saint, to eat at Millennium in San Francisco, to soak in the healing waters of Harbin Hot Springs, to tour the countries and sites of Europe. I can't wait to show you Big Sur. When you are older, I hope to hike the Pacific Crest Trail from Mexico through California to Canada with the three of you. That will be quite a journey, and it inspires me to envision the adventures that lay ahead for us!

My love and respect for nature is something I hope to pass on to you girls. It is important to me that you hold in your hearts a great sentiment and love for our Mother Earth. She is the mother to us all. I want to share with you some day the wilderness vistas that the great naturalist John Muir wrote about. I want to share with you what I know of the beauty that is so abundant and available to us all. I want to watch the expressions come over your faces as that beauty strikes each one of you and thrills your souls.

One of my poems to you reads, "My soul loves your excited smile, you are my sunshine now." The possibility of witnessing your growth and your deepest realizations is the source of my very greatest joy. With that in mind, know this: No judge or court could ever keep me from giving each of you girls absolutely all that I have to give you in this life.

Love always,
All ways.
Dad

The first poem I ever wrote for you girls was shortly after you left for Canada…

From the Moon to the Sea

Naia and Ananda, Jana
Santa Monica, Calif.
April 2010

From the moon to the sea,
You will always be with me.
No matter the time and no matter the place,

I will always see your face,
Hiding in the stars, and shining in the skies,
I will always see your eyes,

And your souls shining through with delight.
So keep smiling,
And laugh!

Every day,
Every night,
There will be good,
And there will be bad,

Just remember I love you always,
Always,
Your Dad.

—Adam Kleinberg

Fred Garbo's Inflatable Theater Company

Ananda, Jana and Naia
239th Street, Riverdale, the Bronx
June 2011

We should consider every day lost on which we have not danced at least once. And we should call every truth false which was not accompanied by at least one laugh.

—Friedrich Nietzsche

January 2011

Dear girls,

As I write, you three girls are visiting New York City for the holidays, here to spend time with your grandmother and me. Earlier today, we went to see a show for children called *Fred Garbo's Inflatable Theater Company* at the Symphony Space Theater. Being at that particular theater with you brought back many vivid memories of my youth in New York City, of my friend Josh and of the exclusive Horace Mann School I attended on an academic scholarship nearly 30 years ago.

On January 9, 1978, exactly 33 years ago to this day, the Upper West Side of Manhattan would begin its embrace of Symphony Space. On that night, the doors were thrust open to a waiting and eager public for a show entitled *Wall to Wall Bach*, the first of the theater's signature 12-hour music marathon events. Another New York City rebirth had begun in a space that was originally opened as a public market at the turn of the century, and then later as an ice skating rink and a boxing arena. In 1931, the Thalia movie theater opened in the same space, and would appear decades later as an homage in *Annie Hall*, one of Woody Allen's many Manhattan-based movies.

I made my first visit to the Thalia when I was 14, accompanied by an interesting and odd friend of mine from Horace Mann. Josh had invited me to his apartment in Manhattan after school one day. His wealthy parents struck me as aloof and cold, and I think he was a bit starved for affection. He took me to see a film he loved, Stanley Kubrick's *A Clockwork Orange*. I don't remember how at our age we managed to get in to the Thalia that day to see the film, but I'm glad we did because seeing that film at such an impressionable young age had a profound effect on me.

Growing up a poor kid in the Bronx had its challenges. In September of 1980, I was thrust into a whole new social order at school with the children of the New York City elite. Of the 900 students that comprised the middle and upper school of Horace Mann, I was one of only a few Caucasian children on academic scholarship—the majority were African American and Hispanic. I can remember our science teacher telling Andrea, the daughter of TV news anchorman Tom Brokaw, that she needed to do her homework regardless of who her father was. It was rumored that my friend Aaron's grandfather gave him a half million in trust for his bar mitzvah, which I attended at the exclusive Pierre Hotel on Fifth Avenue.

Our single mother who was in part relying on welfare at the time was raising my brother and me. She had a part-time job at a diner just a block from our apartment to try to make ends meet. Most mornings I would stop at the diner for some breakfast to go before an hour's journey by two busses going clear across the Bronx from Pelham Parkway to Riverdale. I would then walk up the big steep hill to school with my heavy book bag weighing me down.

Horace Mann was filled with some of the wealthiest kids in the world. My daily amusement would begin by observing the many limousines clogging the streets in front of school each morning. I was not overly impressed by most of my wealthy classmates. Instead, most of my friends were African American and Hispanic, because we were in the same socio-economic group. I rejected the fast track to the Ivy League that Horace Mann could have provided. I remember a day getting thrown out of history class with Josh for the two of us laughing so hard that tears were running down our faces and snot was flying from Josh's nose.

There were a total of about 12 students in our class, and we all sat around a large dark wooden table with our teacher at the helm. The source of our laughter was due to our teacher, Ms. Karanas, being unaware that I was using the lens of my watch to precisely reflect incoming sunlight onto the clothing over her crotch, her nipples and onto the growth on her nose. Bored teenagers will do anything for entertainment, but these are the types of antics that endear junior high school classmates to each other. There is a bond that develops through laughter from rebelling against the establishment, especially at the cost of an authority figure.

Being back at the Symphony Space Theater today made me sentimental for my youth. And what a great show it was! At one time, Fred Garbo was an acrobat performing inside a costume on the TV show *Sesame Street*. He was also the main juggler in the Broadway show *Barnum* that your grandfather Karl took my brother David and me to see more than 30 years ago. Seems Fred has been entertaining me my whole life, and I didn't even know it. But even more important, the joy on your faces today was enough to satisfy any parent for ten thousand lifetimes. If a soundtrack were to accompany the inaugural opening of the gates of heaven, it might just be the sound of your laughter.

I am so grateful to have this time visiting with you. Jana is now 4½ and Naia and Ananda will be 3 in April. I am excited and eager to tell you girls more of the many stories that have shaped my life. I also want you to grow up knowing the principles I stand for and why. In time, my hope is that you will know the things I know with a great depth of understanding and passion. I hope that by honestly revealing myself, I can help you avoid some painful experiences and not have to repeat patterns that kept me from expressing my fullest potential in younger years. I know that if I do my job right, all of our learning together and all of our experiences over the years will be filled with of the kind of laughter we all enjoyed today.

And, as I was a clever class clown, be sure to know that I will keep a close eye on you when the sunlight is shining on your watches —and exactly where you are reflecting it!

Love always,
Dad

Praised One

Ananda, Naia, Jana and Grandmother Judy
Kingston Ontario, Canada
May 2010

The praise that comes from love does not make us vain, but more humble.

—James M. Barrie

June 2012

Dear girls,

The name Judith means "the Praised One." People with this name tend to be passionate, compassionate, intuitive and have magnetic personalities. They are usually humanitarian, broadminded and generous, and follow professions where they can serve humanity. Because they are so affectionate and giving, they may be imposed on frequently. They are romantic and fall in love easily but may be hurt, and are sometimes quick-tempered.

Although it may seem to be highly coincidental, the meaning of the name Judith and the qualities associated with that name are all extraordinarily true about your grandmother. Everybody loves Judy. It's no accident that is her name. She has been a great teacher and mentor in my life. My generosity, passion and dedication to you girls are without a doubt due to the dedication she has given to my brother and me our entire lives.

I feel it is important for you to know more about your grandmother. She has always been there for me like a rock, regardless of the circumstances. She has never let me down whenever I needed support, and she is my role model when it comes to dedication to her children. In my grade school years, I watched her work the breakfast shift at our local Bronx diner for nickels, dimes and quarters. I remember her giving her own dinner away to any friends I spontaneously brought home at dinnertime.

I watched her work her way off of public assistance to become the assistant to the head of Orthopedic Pathology at the esteemed Mount Sinai Hospital on Fifth Avenue on the Upper East Side of Manhattan where she worked for many years. I also remember her visiting me on parent-teacher days at Horace Mann in the early '80s. Every year, students would say, "Wow! Whose mother is that?" She was and still is very beautiful, and I can see her likeness in you girls.

She is still here for me now. No one has given me more help or support in my life. She has endlessly opened her home to me. I stayed at her small apartment with your mom and you girls out of necessity on multiple extended occasions. She gave me gifts that are hard to understand or even put a finger on without consideration that requires deep thought and reflection.

By supporting me the way she did, your grandmother allowed me to experience things that have shaped me and illuminated my spiritual path. She has never stopped believing in me, no matter what the circumstances are, and believe me—I have not made it easy on her! She has always taken on as much of my burden as possible and wanted the best life for me. Her intention is quite selfless.

I recently had a conversation with her and asked her who influenced her to be so selfless. I wanted to know who taught her how to give so much of herself. She had a realization right then and there that it was her own grandmother, Helen. Helen passed the gift of selflessness on to her, Judy has passed it on to me, and I will do everything I can to pass it on to you girls.

Echoing the sentiments of Albert Einstein, the late Dr. Dick Santo who was one of my favorite chiropractic lecturers used to end his talks in part by saying, "The only thing of value is what we do for others." I've always felt that your grandmother put those words into her love and all her actions. I have had a lot of support in many ways from many people in my life to whom I am grateful, but the support from Judy has been unlike any other. She is all of what a parent is supposed to be.

Days will come when you girls will need support from me in different ways. I will always be there to selflessly support you in any way that I can. When I do, always remember that it was your Grandmother Judy's shining example that taught me how to be there for you girls. I know that your mother would wholeheartedly agree.

No one helped me more than Judy when your mother took you girls to Canada. You may not see your grandmother as often as you did when you were younger, now that you live so far away, but it's my hope that you will always feel a growing gratitude for her deep in your hearts. As you girls get older, you will easily recognize how much she deserves it. After all, she is *the praised one*.

Love always,
Dad

Dreams

Naia and Ananda
Wave Hill, Riverdale, the Bronx
July 2011

I dreamt of you last night,
The splendor of your smiles.
I dream of you this day
And feel your love inside.

The light of love surrounds you,
The sun sets in your eyes.
We run through sunflower fields
In the glow of fireflies.

Starlight reveals the river,
Moonbeams outline the trees.
Your silhouettes dance on the shadows
And float down the sweet summer night breeze.

Dream today, dream tomorrow,
Never a care, never a sorrow.

—Adam Kleinberg

The Wilhelmina Talent Agency

Naia and Ananda
Ontario, Canada
September 2011

If you modestly enjoy your fame, you are not unworthy to rank with the holy.

—Johann Wolfgang von Goethe

January 2012

Dear girls,

When my younger brother turned 5 years old, he did a bit of modeling. David was amazingly cute, and his most famous photo was an ad for Bonwit Teller, a high-end department store in New York City. The day they shot the ad, he got to cuddle and snuggle with a stuffed toy elephant bigger than he was. That ad ran in *The New*

York Times Magazine and was a special experience that David is not likely to forget.

In late February 2010, we moved as a family from Santa Cruz to Los Angeles. My logic was that we should be in a place where we could take advantage of as many opportunities as we could. That included opportunities for you three girls in modeling and the film industry.

There are a few factors that made it obvious you would all succeed in the entertainment business. The three of you are quite beautiful, all extroverts and anyone could see that you are friendly, easygoing children. In addition, twins work consistently in film and as models, because of the advantage that one can stand in for the other when needed. With that said, I was getting tired of hearing people constantly compliment you for your good looks and demeanor, many of them suggesting all three of you girls should be modeling. It seemed like a no-brainer! And I wholeheartedly agreed. It was time to do something about it.

Arriving in Los Angeles, we found an agent quite easily. It wasn't a big agency; nevertheless you were enthusiastically sought by the few who saw you. But my LA dream for you fell apart when your mother took you to live in Canada the first week in April, just six weeks after our arrival in LA.

During your summer visit to me in New York in August 2011, I wanted to pursue my dream for you girls and prove there was no doubt about your potential in the entertainment industry. I decided to take you to the two largest and most respected talent agencies for children in the world. I decided we would take a day and go to the Ford agency and then to Wilhelmina, both located in Manhattan. I took special pleasure that day in getting you all ready, dressing you up, brushing your teeth and doing your hair. We wound up first at Wilhelmina on Park Avenue after I lucked out and got a parking space only a block away.

We found our way upstairs and eventually into the agency's

waiting room. While checking in at the front desk, I told the attractive secretary that we did not have an appointment and were a "walk in." I asked her how long it might be to see an agent and told her that we were in no rush. She told me about 40 minutes, so I asked her to tell the agents that the children were adorable, hoping to lessen our wait time. She said, "I already did."

After just a few minutes in the posh waiting area, we were joined by two young and very handsome male models. You three girls decided to make friends with them and they became ample babysitters, obviously entertained by your beauty, friendliness and innocence. You girls then convinced them to show you their portfolios. One of the young men looked like he came right off the page of a Ralph Lauren Polo advertisement. The other looked a lot like Keanu Reeves. It was all great entertainment for me, seeing these two perfect specimens along with the amazing female models that kept coming and going during our wait.

Soon an agent appeared and introduced herself as Teri. She observed the three of you for about 10 seconds and then asked me to me to wait in reception while she took you all back to the children's division. I found it a bit odd to hand you over to a stranger, but Teri seemed trustworthy at first impression. I waited about 15 minutes until her eventual return when she invited me back to join you.

Walking into the open area children's division, I noticed four additional female agents seated around a large communal table. Two of you girls were sitting on agents' laps, getting assistance from them on their respective computers. Another one of you was playing with what appeared to be more than 100 stuffed animals. It seemed as if you three girls had totally won over the hearts of all the agents in the room. Very quickly and for the moment, you had taken over the children's division of the Wilhelmina talent agency.

Teri was lovely and honest. She told me a little about the history of Wilhelmina, her own experience in the business, her position as head of the children's division and what would be necessary to create success for you girls in the business. She offered me her opinion that the twins Naia and Ananda would work non-stop, but she was also incredibly intrigued with Jana. After just a short observation, she commented that Jana was beautiful and "wears every emotion on her face." Teri also solemnly offered me this information: "We never ever invite people on a walk in back here, especially to the children's division, but your girls are incredible." These words were coming straight from one of the most powerful talent agents for children in the world!

What I did not know about Wilhelmina prior to our visit is that they are the only agency to represent children across the board, including stage, print, film and television. I also did not know that Wilhelmina had launched the careers of Natalie Portman, Katherine Heigl and Amanda Seyfried. After a bit more conversation, Teri offered me contracts for all three of you to be represented by Wilhelmina. The only problem was you were not living in New York! The business is obviously very competitive, she explained, and some "go-see" appointments might be scheduled with only a few hours' notice. The agency does ask that parents be dedicated to their kids' careers and get them to all scheduled auditions, regardless of how short the notice may be.

Teri told me to read over the contracts and then get in touch with her to let her know how we wanted to proceed. I left very pleased with confirmation of my overwhelming belief that you girls have a gift that could be met with tremendous opportunity and financial gain for your future schooling and independence as young empowered women. Consequently, we never made it down the street to the Ford agency.

But soon after, my excitement about your potential careers dissipated. After a phone conversation with your mother about our adventure, I was met with anger and irritation. She felt it would be too difficult to travel and possibly relocate due to jobs you might get. Furthermore, she told me I had put her in the difficult predicament of having to explain to you girls in the future why she had turned down the opportunity.

I disagreed with your mother and felt this was an opportunity that should not be taken lightly. I agreed that there are challenging decisions to be made for any parent when deciding to enter their children into the entertainment industry. Wilhelmina, however, is no rinky-dink, Mickey Mouse talent agency. We are talking about one of the largest, most powerful and reputable agencies in all of entertainment, and the head of the children's division was in love with you three girls.

Your mother and I both agree that you girls need to be protected from the sick and demented things that happen in the world we live in, but we differ in our opinion about getting you into the entertainment industry. You are at an age where the work would not affect you on an egoic level. It could all be fun and innocent, like it was for your uncle David, and it is likely that it would not last forever. It is not my goal to see you as big Hollywood stars someday, although if you had your heads on straight, that would be fine with me.

I do, however, want you all to have financial independence as young women with a head start to make your way in the world. Employment through Wilhelmina could mean five- and six-figure incomes for you, which is literally a ridiculous amount of money for the work involved, and all you would have to do is be yourselves. While I believe it is the responsibility of your mother and I to provide you with a financial head start through our own efforts, I believe it is also our job to recognize the gifts you have been given and manage how those gifts can serve you best.

Considering your mother did recently adorn the cover of *Pregnancy Magazine*, walked the runway in Canada for potential agents and was bursting to pursue her own modeling career, I thought that this opportunity was not something to be trivialized.

Further confirmation for pursuing this path arrived a few days after our trip to Wilhelmina when we were invited to go swimming at the home of an old family friend named Jay. Jay's friend Marc Sarfati stopped by for a short visit to say hello. It just so happens that Marc's daughter is Lea Michele, the star of the television show *Glee*.

Sitting around the pool, we got to chatting about our kids, and he told me a little about how Lea got started, how she was dealing with her current fame, and how she confides in him when making decisions in her life and career. I told him the story about our trip to Wilhelmina and the potential opportunity that resulted. He watched you girls in the pool with your floaties and rafts, and your blonde hair shining in the mid-August sunshine. Although he is a Spanish Sephardic Jew, Marc said to me in a mild Bronx/Italian accent, "From what I'm looking at here, you would have to be crazy not to take that opportunity."

Once again, I wholeheartedly agreed. There is a window open now while you girls are young that will narrow with complications as you get older, and Marc, as a father who'd been down this road, was urging me to step up to the challenge now.

Returning home, I called Teri at Wilhelmina and spoke with her about the situation of you three living in Canada. She told me the busy season is May through mid-August and that she would be happy to work with us within that timeframe. I resolved to do all I could to give you this opportunity—at least for one season—to see where it might lead.

Right now, your height and your level of talent don't matter. As you get older, there will be more competition and other factors that can make it more difficult to open a door like the one that is now open. I will keep my intention focused and pure for you to have the success in this endeavor that you deserve.

It is my feeling that you deserve to know about the opportunity that may shape your future. The rewards are too great to be ignored. But I want you to know that regardless of the outcome, the three of you will always be the biggest and brightest stars shining in my sky.

Love you always,
Dad

Jana. Our day at Wilhelmina…
August 2011

Part II
Love, Love, Love

Jana, age 4
Santa Monica, Calif.
April 2010

Gift from God: Dedication to Jana

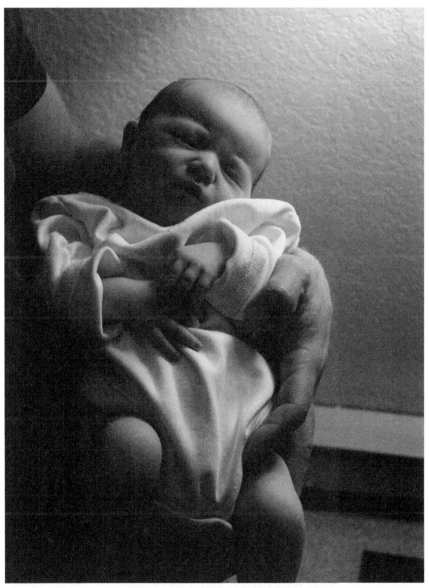

Jana in my arms at 4 days old
San Mateo, Calif.
May 16, 2006

To my gift from God,
That is what the name "Jana" means.

May 2006

Dear Jana,

You are only one week old as I write to you today. Your name means, "gift from God," and so you are. Your mother and I are amazed but not surprised at your symmetry, your beauty and your sovereignty. We are very proud that against strong societal and familial opposition we birthed you at home without professional assistance. Your mother had the faith in herself and in me to allow you the non-violent and drug-free birth that all children deserve. She is an amazing woman. We believe that there is an innate intelligence within us all, and as B. J. Palmer, one of the founders of the chiropractic profession said, "Nature needs no help—just no interference."

Through this process of pregnancy and birth, I have learned that true objectivity is scarce among humanity, but to deviate from one's principles due to the pressure of the majority is the destruction of one's freedom. People more often operate out of a state of fear and doubt rather than from a state of confidence and abundance.

I could never have known before you arrived what the gift of parenthood and the blessing of a child would feel like. My heart is overwhelmed with joy, gratitude and humility. As I reflect on my life, I realize that it has been a continuous search for truth. I have also realized that the keys to my personal freedom have been the books I chose to read. They have become my most valued possessions. Someday as you reflect on this, your birth dedication, I hope your study of those books has pointed you towards mystical realizations of your own about the nature of reality and the secrets of the universe.

Some of the greatest spiritual masters, mystics, writers, poets, quantum physicists and former academics-turned-bohemian have advised me to treat you as my equal. They have also revealed to me that you are my greatest teacher, although you are a just a beautiful helpless infant right now. Most importantly, they have pointed out how simple it is to recognize your divinity. I have chosen to whole-heartedly follow their advice.

The word "inspiration" has several meanings. One is, *divine guidance or influence exerted directly on the mind and soul*. Another definition is *arousal of the mind to special extraordinary activity or creativity*. I hope to be one of your greatest inspirations. If I can be an instrument to help you express your greatest potential, I will have fulfilled my own.

I have found that inspiration of magnificence comes with the perseverance of being true to oneself. There is true liberty in the disciplined path of the great minority, as Robert Frost pointed to when he wrote, "Two roads diverged in a wood, and I—I took the one less traveled by, and that has made all the difference" in his poem "The Road Not Taken."

So Jana Aum, always follow your ideals. As you become the master of yourself, you will realize that ideals are worth living for and perhaps even dying for. You should always know that happiness is a state of being that you create from within and is not something that anything outside yourself can bring. Recognize the divinity and One-ness within yourself and all other things, and you will transcend much of the suffering that comes along with being human. Most of all, know that love is the greatest ideal, and love is what you were created from. As I write this letter to you, there is a great deal of joy inside my tears.

All my love,
Dad

I Love You All the Way to Heaven

The words that became the title of this poem were spoken to me by Jana one day, and now you three girls and I say them to each other all the time…

Jana, age 1
Pleasanton, Calif.
May 2007

I love you all the way to Heaven,
And around the moon too.
I love you in your rainbow dress,
I love you in one shoe.

I love you when the sun is bright,
And when we're at the sea,
Inside your heart I see the light,
You're a little piece of me.

I love you in the pink sunset,
I love you to the sky,
I love you when your hair is wet,
I even love you when you cry.

I love you when you are laughing loud,
I love when you say, *Wow!*
My soul loves your excited smile,
You are my sunshine now.

I love to watch you in your sleep,
And when you hug me tight.
I love you when you want a treat,
And when we fly a kite.

The love you have inside your heart,
Is quite simple to see,
I feel that love shine through your eyes,
And your love flows through me.

—Adam Kleinberg

Angel Twins:
Dedication to Naia and Ananda

Naia and Ananda
Burlingame Calif.
April 2008

Naia means to flow, to blossom, water goddess and nymph
Ananda means bliss or delight

One would have been enough to satisfy the desires of any father.
One would have been enough to fill my heart with infinite gratitude.
One would have been enough to bring my life more joy than I had ever
thought possible.
And I was given two…

—Dad

April 16, 2008

Dear Naia and Ananda,

Your mother and I live a very natural lifestyle; you might even call us "naturalists" if you were to put a label on how we live. That being said, we allowed very little testing to be done during your mother's pregnancy with you and as a result had only a sneaking suspicion that there were two of you. We did not mention this suspicion to our midwife, due to the fact that we would have been forced into a hospital birth had it been known. She was the professional, and with Doppler radar as her only tool, even she couldn't find Ananda hiding behind Naia and upside down in the womb.

After Naia had emerged, the midwife's assistant told your mother that the other thing your mother was feeling inside her was the placenta. Your mother's composed response to her was, "Placentas don't have elbows." Exactly 15 minutes later, Ananda arrived.

And then there were two of you. You were early, and because twins are considered an emergency procedure, we were all rushed to San Francisco General Hospital in two ambulances. I had to focus on every detail of your care to preserve the integrity of our decisions for you. After nearly 48 hours of being awake, I could finally rest, knowing that my wishes for you would be granted. You were both so beautiful and perfect, every doctor and nurse commented on how amazing and accelerated your progress was.

They kept you both in the hospital for 10 days, and your mother and I could not wait to get you home to shield you from the negative influences of the conventional American medical model. As a Doctor of Chiropractic, I have a very different philosophy from and mostly the opposite of conventional Western medicine.

When it comes to emergencies, modern medicine does an amazing job of treatment, sometimes bordering on the miraculous. However, in non-emergencies it is a different story. According to a Canadian study highlighted in USA Today in 2009, a low-risk home birth is statistically twice as safe as delivering in a hospital. According to the Center for Disease Control (CDC) website, home births rose in the U.S. by nearly 30 percent over the years 2004-2009. This situation you'd think would be enough to discourage hospital birth, but my other grievance with hospitals is that they commonly harbor superbugs that breed on the diseased and dying. The illnesses that result are now referred to as *hospital acquired infections* or HAIs. Garbage brings rats. Rats don't bring garbage.

Your progress after being born was phenomenal, which came as no surprise to your mother and me. We have the utmost confidence in the lifestyle we have chosen. You both had your first chiropractic adjustments at one hour old; I could feel Naia's atlas—her first cervical vertebra just under the skull—move under a very light pressure from my pinky finger. When you are older, I will tell you some of the stories of my oppression as a wellness-based chiropractor, including how some of the doctors at the hospital disapproved of the care I would give to my own newborn daughters as a licensed Doctor of Chiropractic! I would have cut them all down with a Samurai sword to get my hands on your tiny, newborn spines, but I was very glad I didn't have to resort to any pleas. (The importance of the adjustment I did on Naia is explained in detail in a later letter in the book that is all about chiropractic.)

Your mother and I want to raise you in a unique way. We do not acquiesce to the conventional or popular pseudo-science propaganda that most of America is misled into. We cannot ignore the wisdom we have sought and found. We know that we will give you an amazing start to life if we can stick to our principles.

Your mother gained only 28 pounds during her pregnancy with you, and you were both well ahead of average weight at birth. She ate when she was hungry, and you got everything you needed. What an amazing concept! Your mother and I like to think of ourselves as the "myth-busters," in that we didn't fall for so many of the false beliefs that are hoisted upon new parents. Just like your sister

Jana, you will be raised with regular chiropractic adjustments, and you will be raised in a vegetarian/vegan lifestyle—not exactly the conventional approach, but what our experience has proven to us as best.

I look forward to the day when you can understand all the choices we make for you. It has taken me 40 years to free myself from so much of what I was led to believe and to become truly objective in my thought process. It is my deepest yearning that when you are old enough to make your own decisions you will adopt the philosophies that your mother and I have fought so hard for.

There is a path that leads to true joy and happiness, and you will come to realize someday that that path is your natural state. When we look at the two of you now, you are experientially blank slates, perhaps even *tabula rasa*. You are pure expressions of the Divine Universal Intelligence personified. You are both so naturally full of joy as long as you are loved, fed and your diapers changed.

The qualities you can always expect from me in our relationship are openness, honesty, integrity, kindness, gentleness and a tremendous amount of love. I hope to receive the same from you. I will do everything in my power to help you get the most out of your life, and I hope that the deep love and respect we develop for each other will be an example to you both for what is possible in any relationship.

Know that your freedom, true freedom, only comes when you learn how to think for yourself and when you learn how to believe in your own ideals, no matter how overwhelming the opposition may seem. Many wise people have declared, *The journey is more rewarding than the destination*. I would also say that when you fight for what you know is right for you, you are living the highest of ideals.

So Naia Aum and Ananda Aum, don't ever forget how much I love you. Always guard in your heart that love is the highest ideal and know that love is the source you were created from. Thank you for joining us here on earth and for already being such brightly shining stars in a weary world.

All my love,
Always,
Dad

True Friends

Naia and Ananda
Kingston, Ontario Canada
May 2011

Yesterday brought the beginning, tomorrow brings the end,
And somewhere in the middle we became the best of friends.
—Anonymous

December 2011

Dear girls,

My oldest friend, someone I knew from the day I was born, is a man named Greg Botnick. Greg is the same age as I am, and as a baby he survived a five-story fall from a terrace with very few and relatively trivial physical consequences. The story of his life is a miracle and a tragedy at the same time. When we graduated from grade school at age 12, he wrote something special in my graduation book that I remember to this day: *I met you as a friend, I kept you as a friend, I hope we meet in heaven, where friendship never ends.* We are still true friends to this day.

I have been thinking a lot about friends lately and wanted to share with you my thoughts about friendship. True friends are hard to come by. There are many people you will come across in your life who you may think are your friends, and there are many people who will call themselves your friends, but very few of them will actually be your true friends.

A true friend is someone who always has your best interest at heart. A true friend is there for you when times are good and when times are bad. A true friend will always try to bring you up, not bring you down. A true friend will not try to make you do things you really don't want to do. By this I don't mean anything trivial like dragging you to a movie you really don't want to see, but I do mean things that are against your ethics and morals.

A true friend will always look out for you even when you are not looking out for yourself. A true friend will always be honest with you even if it might hurt your feelings and even if you don't want to hear what they have to say. A true friend will share with you. A true friend will encourage you. A true friend will never be jealous of you but will always be happy for you.

Pick your friends carefully. Trust is something that your friends should have to earn from you over time. If you trust a friend too much too soon, that person might break your heart. Try not to choose friends you can't learn from or who bring you down. Try not to choose friends who don't respect themselves. If they don't respect themselves, how can they respect you or anyone else? Try not to choose friends who are overly dramatic, who are accusatory or who tend to pressure you.

Your friend's actions and deeds should make you proud of them. Your friends should be happy without a reason and should always try to look at the positive side of life. Your true friends should be able to say anything to you and be able to listen to anything you need to say to them. You will not always agree, but that will never come between you if you are true friends.

Your true friends should support you in all the things that matter to you. A true friend will compromise with you, so you can both be happy with your decisions and with the activities you want to share together. True friends will not embarrass you purposefully and will protect you when you need it. A true friend will never rat you out but will confront you about things you do that are wrong.

A true friend will be there to share your greatest accomplishments and your worst tragedies. A true friend will treat your family like her own, will respect them and want only the best for all the people you love and care about. A true friend won't be jealous of your relationships with other people and will never get between you and your other friends.

Hopefully you will have a group of tight-knit, true friends because everybody needs that kind of friendship. The true friends you make will be your friends for life. You are never too young or too old to make a new friend. A true friend will love you. When necessary, a true friend will put your needs before her own.

As you grow up, you will encounter popular people who seem to have a lot of friends. Don't believe it! The cult of celebrity has fair weather friends, pretenders and posers who disappear when times get rough. Oprah Winfrey wisely pointed this out when she said,

"Lots of people want to ride with you in the limo, but what you want is someone who will take the bus with you when the limo breaks down."

Never feel guilty about not embracing someone as your friend. Be polite and be kind, but never feel pressured to be friends with someone. Choose carefully whom you choose to spend time with and whom you let into your inner circle. You become what you surround yourself with.

Being a true friend to someone is a lot of responsibility, and you should not take it lightly. Always remember, the best way to make a true friend and to keep a good friend is to be a good friend. It is important to remember that even your best friends will make mistakes that will hurt you and themselves in life. When you have a true friend, you may not see each other or speak for many years, depending on what is happening in your lives. When you do see each other again, it will be right as rain, and although you may look different, have different jobs, have families of your own and different philosophies, the bond that you have as true friends will always be eternal.

The humanitarian Albert Schweitzer wrote, "In everyone's life, at some time, our inner fire goes out. It is then burst into flame by an encounter with another human being. We should all be thankful for those people who rekindle the inner spirit."

Although I am your father, I am also your true friend, and a truer friend you will never find. I am wishing for you an abundance of positive, loving, intelligent and unique true friends to come into your life. Remember to be true friends to each other as sisters and, perhaps most importantly, remember to treat yourself like a true friend would treat you. Nothing could make me happier.

Love always,
Dad

Connection

Jana and me
Burlingame, Calif.
May 2008

I feel you:
When I'm still in deep silence.

Eyes shut,
I see you in my mind's eye,
You're the love behind my smile.

I feel your tiny hands grasping mine.
I hear your chuckle, your sweet, untroubled laughter.
I smell the innocent bouquet of your hair.

I can see your life at light speed,
First kiss, stargazing,
Your search for truth and beauty.

Invite joy and light into your life.
Turn a blind, uninterested eye to darkness and worry.
Allow your heart to be open.

Keep your soul clean,
Be kind,
And be happy Goddesses of the Universe.

—Adam Kleinberg

Love Letter

Naia and Ananda
August 2011

Certain it is that there is no kind of affection so purely angelic as of a father to a daughter. In love to our wives, there is desire; to our sons, ambition; but to our daughters, there is something which there are no words to express.

—Joseph Addison

March 2012

Dear girls,

I love you girls so much it hurts!

It hurts because I know that your future will hold inevitable disappointments and heartbreak for you, just like it does for all people. This is the destiny of a father who loves his daughters. I know the best ways I can show you just how much I love you are to help you minimize the hurtful parts of your lives, and to give you as much patience and support as I can.

I feel a tremendous responsibility to you as your father, especially now that your mother and I are no longer together, and at present I am not a part of your everyday lives. This is our karma—what life has given us—and I do my very best to remain grateful for it. It is not easy all the time so I try to focus on just the blessing of being your father and that alone can be enough to keep my heart overflowing with abundance. These are not just words to try to ease the potential heartache over the fact that we no longer live together, but the result of hard emotional work and spiritual growth. I have found abundance in the state of non-attachment. Having to curb my emotional attachment to you, as well as to outcomes I cannot control, eases my own suffering, and has resulted in a staggering growth phase in my life.

I like to use the analogy of myself as the rocket boosters of a space shuttle, carrying the ship to break through the gravity of our planet's atmosphere. Once the boosters use all their energy to propel the shuttle into space, they fall away, totally spent and discarded. The shuttle then takes the next step of exploration into uncharted territory, but it could never have gotten there without the boosters. I am proud to have been chosen to guide you, protect you and raise you. I yearn for nothing more than to see you live your lives free and with joy. It will be an honor to introduce you to some tools to help you see that freedom and joy is within.

I am not an enlightened Buddha though. I am still human flesh, bones and emotion. And in that humanity, there is love, the love only a father can have for his precious daughters. This is the kind of love that includes attachment to the outcome of your lives. It is a very self-ish love because any pain you feel will cause me pain. But it is a pain I am willing to bear to a great degree because I accept my worldly responsibility as your father. However, the love that has no attachment to any outcome is a much deeper one.

The love of non-attachment celebrates each moment of your existence. In the love of non-attachment, I can be in a state of complete joy, grace and gratitude without any attachment to what may come in the future. In the short time you three girls have been in my life, you have already become my greatest teachers. You have taught me unconditional love. You have taught me kindness and gentleness. You definitely continue to teach me patience every day!

Most importantly, I look forward to simply sharing life with you. There is ultimate joy for me in the simple moments of joy in your lives. It is in the little things that I find such joy, like the four of us eating a meal together or the expression of your amusement when hearing the lyrics of a song. Jana was recently tickled over the lyrics from Paul Simon's *Fifty Ways to Leave Your Lover*. The words hit her funny bone and within minutes all three of you were laughing hysterically over those words on our long ride from New York back to Canada.

The very hardest part for me of being away from you girls is not being able to put my healing hands on you when you need healing adjustments the most. I know that there is no other person in the entire world who could match the potential of love, healing and intention that comes through my hands when I care for you. Because I am your father, we have that connection that endures across all time and space. My healing energy is always available to you, even when we are far apart.

The love I have for you girls is also the love of being your friend. I will always be honest with you and hope to gain your trust through my own honesty. I will never punish you for remaining honest with me. Why should you be punished for making the same mistakes that all people do? I would rather work together with you to replace self-harming actions with self-respecting and honorable ones. I will keep my heart open to you with a singular focus on accepting you as you are. I will, however, also do my best to inspire you with passions of my own and to introduce them to you along the way. There is so much I want to show you. There is so much to see, and there is always so much to learn.

The 17th century poet Robert Herrick wrote, *Gather ye rosebuds while ye may, Old Time is still a-flying; and this same flower that smiles today, To-morrow will be dying.* What he meant is what I want to tell you: Live your life without regret. Live with passion and don't take life for granted, not for one minute. The grandeur of youth is the feeling of invincibility. The wisdom of the ages is learning to let go of the attachment to any outcome.

Sometimes I wonder how I could possibly grow to love you girls anymore than I do now. I guess the answer to that will come in time. In one of my many favorite films, *The Notebook*, the main character Noah says, "The best love is the kind that awakens the soul and makes us reach for more, that plants a fire in our hearts and brings peace to our minds, and that's what you've given me."

And that is precisely what you precious girls have given me. You have awakened my soul. Thank you for filling my life with meaning and purpose.

Love always,
Dad

Jana, age 2½
Dublin, Ireland
2009

Part III
Wellness for Body, Mind and Spirit

Ananda and Naia, age 3
Bronx, N.Y.
August 2011

Meditation Is Your Best Medication

Jana, age 1
San Mateo, Calif.
May 2007

Honor your Self. Worship your Self. Meditate on your Self.
God dwells within you, as you.

—Swami Muktananda

April 2011

Dear girls,

Many of the best moments alone in my life, moments that I have been my happiest, have come during meditation. These moments have allowed me to experience a potentially limitless clarity, but just that glimpse into the infinite can touch the soul so deeply that in an instant one's life can take on an entirely new meaning. Meditation has touched my life as profoundly as I believe any experience could possibly do.

Some of the most successful people in the world are passionate advocates of meditation. This list of *Who's Who* includes author Jack Canfield who is the co-creator of the mega successful *Chicken Soup for the Soul* series, musician Paul McCartney who may have had a hit or two over the last five decades with the Beatles, Wings and his solo career, and the hip-hop mega-producer and author Russell Simmons. The author, doctor and health guru Deepak Chopra was also an early inspiration for me regarding meditation. His books *Perfect Health, Return of the Rishi* and the blockbuster *Ageless Body, Timeless Mind* made a great impression on me as a young man, molding my world view.

I started meditating about 17 years ago. I had been interested in learning how to meditate for many years before that, but I had a very hard time finding any books at the library that would teach me a method of meditation. Believe it or not, that was before the Internet. (Somehow, writing how the Internet was not in mass usage at an earlier point in my life makes me feel ancient!)

While attending university from 1996 to 2000, I worked at the Sakura Japanese restaurant in Westport, Conn. In those years smoking was still legal in restaurants, and I would bare the brunt of the smoke at the bar in exchange for the almighty dollar. My dad Karl and I used to bartend together there on Saturday nights while I put myself through chiropractic school. One of our regular customers, a heavy drinker and obviously wealthy man, ended up one evening in a conversation with me about meditation. I suppose I was surprised to be conversing with him about anything like meditation, as he seemed to be living an unhealthy life of excess. Just goes to prove once again that you can't judge a book by its cover.

I had looked into the Transcendental Meditation program several times but could not afford it. After gauging my sincerity and passion about wanting to learn to meditate, this man who barely knew me paid nearly $2,000 for me to go through the program with my girlfriend Lee. This man has no idea that what he gave me turned out to be one of the greatest gifts I have ever received. On the other hand, maybe he knew all along that it would be. Meditation is precious to me. I hope that someday soon it will be to you girls as well.

Trying to explain the essence of meditation is like trying to write a poem about existence itself. It is not an easy task. Alan Watts, the author and Zen master who popularized Buddhism and meditation in the West in the 1950s, is quoted as saying the following:

> We could say that meditation doesn't have a reason or doesn't have a purpose. In this respect it's unlike almost all other things we do except perhaps making music and dancing. When we make music we don't do it in order to reach a certain point, such as the end of the composition. If that were the purpose of music then obviously the fastest players would be the best. Also, when we are dancing we are not aiming to arrive at a particular place on the floor as in a journey. When we dance, the journey itself is the point, as when we play music the playing itself is the point. And exactly the same thing is true in meditation. Meditation is the discovery that the point of life is always arrived at in the immediate moment.

I practice two main forms of meditation, one passive and the other active. The passive meditation I practice is Transcendental Meditation, or as it is more popularly known, TM. The history of TM began when Maharishi Mahesh Yogi started teaching it in India in the late 1950s. The first organizations established to teach TM in the USA were the Spiritual Regeneration Movement and the International Meditation Society. In this type of meditation, a mental tool called a *mantra* is utilized to raise self-awareness and to help the meditator become aware of becoming lost in thought.

Although it was not the mantra assigned to me by my teacher when I first started practicing TM, I now use the mantra *Aum (Om) Namah Shivaya*. It is said that this mantra is used to call upon the energy of transformation and destruction, or Shiva, a Hindu God known as the destroyer or transformer. Shiva is called upon to burn away all attachments to free a person to experience a connection between individual consciousness and the greater consciousness, or the One.

The *Bhagavad-Gita* is an ancient Sanskrit scripture that explains how the ordinary person falsely experiences him or herself to be an individual soul within an individual body. This limited point of view leads to considerable suffering as we think of only our individual problems, becoming distracted from the higher reality of Oneness that is our birthright. Day to day, we live under the illusion that our individual experience is the whole of reality. As we practice meditation to help detach ourselves from this illusion, we find ourselves awakening to a much more expansive reality. We experience a wonderful compassion for fellow sentient beings. The fear of death loses its power.

Sages declare that mantra is life, that mantra is action, that mantra is love and that the repetition of mantra bursts forth wisdom from within. When I begin to meditate each morning, I sit crossed-legged in a quiet place with my eyes closed, and focus on my breath to allow myself to relax and surrender to the "Now." Sometimes, I lie on my back in corpse pose also known as *Shavasana* (from the Sanskrit) with arms and legs spread. This is also known as the anatomical position made most famous by Leonardo da Vinci in his work *Vitruvian Man.*

I gently repeat my mantra in my mind with ease. Thoughts will naturally creep in during meditation; that is expected. As you become more experienced in meditation, it will become easier for you to be an observer of yourself and of your own mind. It will become much easier to realize when your mind has slipped away from your mantra and back into thought. Eckhart Tolle, author of *The Power of Now* and *A New Earth,* cleverly calls this process "watching the thinker."

When you have the realization that you are thinking, you can gently move away from your thoughts and return to your mantra. It is really that simple. The repetition of this cycle is the essence of Transcendental Meditation. You become lost in thought and then you transcend that thought to move into a higher state of awareness. I like to think, in a way, that meditation is a brief daily surrender of your life with its worries and problems into a pure, open, aware state of being. Your heart opens, your mind expands into the infinite Oneness, and you can have deep realizations about the nature of reality and who you really are. It is something uniquely experiential that no one can ever take away from you. I practice this meditation first thing each morning when I wake up for about 30 minutes. It is a pure blessing teaching you girls how to meditate. We have had several sessions already.

There are a lot of books that have been extremely influential in strengthening my meditation practice and opening my heart. Swami Muktananda's book *Meditate: Happiness Lies Within* had a huge influence on me. Other books that have been equally inspirational are Sri Chinmoy's *Eastern Light for the Western Mind* and *Meditation: Man Perfection in God-Satisfaction,* Swami Rama's *Meditation and Its Practice,* and Maharishi Mahesh Yogi's *Science of Being and Art of Living: Transcendental Meditation.* There are many others as well that you will be able to find in your future library!

The other type of meditation that I practice is an active meditation. A great man named Dr. Sid Williams taught this to me. Dr. Williams was the founder of Life University, the largest chiropractic university in the world. At a quarterly seminar that I would attend loyally, Dr. Sid would often lead between one and two thousand people in a large group meditation. He will never be forgotten.

This active type of meditation has three parts that are repeated in a cycle: spoken affirmations, diaphragmatic breathing and Aum chanting. The breathing portion is called *Bhastrika Pranayama*. This is a technique of forceful breath in the nose and out the mouth. Bhastrika Pranayama is aimed at keeping the inhalation breath equal to exhalation while making the breath deeper and longer. I do this meditation seated with my legs crossed, my palms turned up on my knees for the affirmations and turned down for the breaths and chanting. I follow my passive TM practice each morning with this active meditation. It also lasts about 30 minutes.

The spoken affirmations can consist of any words you choose. The words I use regularly are *light, love, peace, joy, grace, abundance, wisdom* and *gratitude*. The affirmation is as follows: *I am light, I am filled with light, every cell of my being is filled with light. I do not have to become light, I am already light, right now, this moment, I am light.* I follow that with three diaphragmatic breaths that are fast, deep and vigorous on the inhale and the exhale. Diaphragmatic breathing expands the belly as the diaphragm descends, inhaling through the nose and exhaling through the mouth. I then follow that with three equally deep diaphragmatic inhalations and chant *Aum* on the exhalation of each breath.

This sequence of spoken words, diaphragmatic breaths and Aum chanting is then repeated, substituting the different words through the cycle and building the breaths up from 3 to 7 to 14 to 21 and back down to 14 to 7 to 3 and then 1. The Aum chanting follows the breaths and remains at three chants throughout each word of the cycle. The Aum chanting is through a long, slow exhale with focus on separating the word into three sounds, *Aaah-Ohhhh-Mmmm*, and projecting the sounds to the third eye (in the middle of the forehead), the throat and the heart, respectively. The sound should resonate in these energy centers known as *chakras*.

When chanting, each syllable of Aum is of equivalent length. The *Aaah* should be with the mouth wide open. The *Ohhhh* should be with lips pursed in a circle. The *Mmmm* should be with the bottom and top teeth gently clenched and lips closed, which causes a vibration throughout the skeletal system of the body and a resonation in the central nervous system. Stephen Gaskin wrote about this vibration in his book *Cannabis Spirituality*. In my personal experience, each Aum chant may last from 10 to nearly 30 seconds.

The chart below summarizes how to do this form of active meditation.

Flow Chart for Active Meditation in 8 Cycles		
Spoken Affirmation➜	Pranayama Breaths➜	Aum Chanting➜ (REPEAT)
"I am light," etc.➜ Breathe in the nose and out the mouth➜ Deep Inhale, Ah, Oh, Mm ➜(REPEAT)		
Affirmation Word	Number of Breaths	Number of Aum Chants
1. Light	3	3
2. Love	7	3
3. Peace	14	3
4. Joy	21	3
5. Grace	14	3
6. Abundance	7	3
7. Wisdom	3	3
8. Gratitude	1	1
FINISH-		

There's no need to judge yourself in meditation or feel like you need to accomplish something. Part of the benefit of meditation comes just from being disciplined and devoted enough to do it every day. Sometimes you will be rushed but even a few minutes of meditation can make a world of difference. After 17 years, I still find myself lost in thought at some point in every meditation. Once again that is natural. The intervals have shortened in the time it takes for me to realize that I am thinking, and the duration of time that I am without thought has improved and evolved to bring more depth and freedom.

The spoken affirmations are literally creating physical beauty and regeneration. I have seen a great confirmation of the principle that thoughts and intentions manifest into reality by the work of Dr. Masaru Emoto, author of *The Hidden Messages in Water*. His research was presented exquisitely in the movie *What the Bleep Do We Know?* Positive and negative words are placed on bottles of water. Dr. Emoto then presents pictures of the microscopic water crystals as they freeze. The difference in images from the beauty of the positive crystals to the ugliness of the negative ones is indisputable. It is like comparing diamonds with lumps of coal. Do not doubt the science behind meditation. There are more than 600 studies done in 30 of the most prestigious institutions in the world that support the multitude of health benefits of the Transcendental Meditation method alone!

Many years ago, your grandmother Judy was diagnosed with high blood pressure—high enough to be categorized as hypertension. She stopped using the drug she was taking because it made her violently ill in just three days. I pleaded with her to try meditation to see if it would help her. After 30 days of meditation and no other habit changes, her blood pressure was back to 115/78, which is spot on. I would say to her every day, "Meditation is your best medication," and we would laugh.

The diaphragmatic breathing in this active meditation invigorates the body by oxygenating the tissues and stimulating the internal organs. In his book *The Science of Breath*, Swami Rama writes:

> *Breath awareness strengthens the mind and makes it easier for it to become inward. When the mind starts*

following the flow of the breath, one becomes aware of the reality that all the creatures of the world are breathing the same breath. There is a direct communication between the student and that center of the cosmos, which supplies breath to all living creatures.

He later states:

Meditation is the sustained state of one-pointedness of mind. In deep meditation, the one-pointed mind is able to pierce through the layers of the conscious and unconscious minds to the super-conscious state. This breakthrough is called Samadhi. On achieving it, one is freed from all bondage and transcends the limitations of time, space, and causation. The microcosm expands to become the macrocosm, just as a drop of water merges with the ocean and becomes the ocean. The individual Atman is united with, and achieves total identity with, the cosmic Brahman. Such a one has found the kingdom of God within himself and has won the ultimate freedom—freedom from the endless chain of birth and death. The evolution of man to God is now complete.

I have had what I believe to be brief instances or momentary glimpses of this state, but just those moments have been enough to confirm that I discovered a wonderful path. I hope you can find this type of grace and much more in your own lives, and all my love is directing you there. Aum is the most often chanted sound among all the sacred sounds on earth. This sound is considered as the sound of existence itself. It is believed that the whole universe, in its fundamental form, is made up of vibrating, pulsating energy. Aum is considered as the humming sound of this cosmic energy, and chanting Aum is a way to align your being with it. The fact that Aum is the middle name all three of you girls share is no coincidence. I hope your common name will be a bond for you throughout your lives.

According to quantum physics, your material body is just an illusion. It is an organized energy moving so fast that it gives the appearance of being solid. In actuality, the fundamental particles that make up your body and all other material things are empty space. You are empty space! In 2009, I met Dr. Bruce Lipton in Santa Cruz at a screening of the documentary *The Living Matrix* that he is featured in. I love his work and he wrote about this quantum concept with unique perspective and clarity in his amazing debut book *The Biology of Belief.*

You are part of the fabric of organized energy that makes up and connects everything in the universe. This is my personal view of what is "God," a matrix of One-energy that comprises the entirety of existence. This concept is based on the Hindu view from the sacred Sanskrit writings known as the *Vedas.* Your physical body is also a manifestation of energy points called *chakras.* In English, the word *chakra* means "whirling vortices of light." Always remember that you *are* light. Always remember that you *are* love. You are the wisdom of the ages of the entire universe, my sweet daughters. To quote the Indian philosopher, author, social revolutionary, poet, composer and linguist Shrii Shrii Anandamurti: *You are never alone or helpless. The force that guides the stars guides you, too.*

I have faith that you will fully discover and practice meditation in your daily life, and help others find the path to meditation and greater self-discovery. I can't imagine that there will be many things I can share with you in life that will be as important. In the meantime, I will meditate on a future where you share with your children and grandchildren the same love, passion and understanding of meditation that I am sharing with you now. It is more important now than ever. It is time to build a vast army of love warriors. Peace on Earth is the plan.

Love always,
Dad

Naia, age 3
Ontario, Canada
September 2011

Unique

You are incredibly unique!
More elegant than orchids,
More elaborate than snowflakes,
Like the sunrise, you are timeless.

The stars gave birth to you,
The oceans bathe you,
The winds will raise you,
The mountains watch over you.

Oh, children full of wonder
Bless your open hearts!
The grace to watch you blossom
Is the gift of my karma.

My love for you is perennial;
My soul is with you always.

—Adam Kleinberg

You Are What You Eat

Jana, me, Ananda and Naia
Santa Cruz, Calif.
April 2009

Let food be your medicine.
—Hippocrates

November 2010

Dear Girls,

When I was in my junior year of high school I started to do a lot of weight lifting. My buddies and I wanted big muscles and lots of them because we figured that was the best way to get girls interested. Boys at that age do just about everything with the sole purpose of getting girls interested.

Like most teenagers in the mid '80s, I knew nothing about nutrition. On one occasion, after an intense two-hour weightlifting session, my friend Greg and I were starved and stopped by our local bodega to buy a couple of Heinekens that we snuck into McDonald's. I wish this were not true, but while illegally enjoying my beers, I ate a Big Mac, a Quarter Pounder, a Filet O Fish, a large French fries and a nine-piece Chicken McNuggets. And that was only 30 minutes before I went home to have dinner.

Grandma Judy would routinely have dinner ready at six o'clock, and that night dinner included a steak, baked potato, broccoli, a piece of apple pie and a big glass of milk. My friends and I were only interested in ingesting as many calories as possible, so we ate like animals, willingly and naively buying into the popular myth that we need so much more protein than we actually do. Humans need protein the most in infancy to thrive and grow. Breast milk, which is the perfect food for an infant, is only 5-10 percent protein. We need much less protein as adults than we have been led to believe.

Later in my early 20s, I became a foodie, which was easy with the array of fine dining restaurants that New York City had to offer. My favorite steakhouse was in Brooklyn, and my favorite seafood house was on City Island in the Bronx. My friends and I ate at iconic Manhattan restaurants, and although I had started to cut fatty foods out of my diet, back then I would still laugh at and ridicule vegetarianism.

Looking back a bit further to when I was about 14, I had grown addicted to the act of eating itself. If I had grown up in this day and age, I would certainly have been obese. I remember eating whole salamis, entire boxes of cookies and up to 24 Kraft American cheese slices in one sitting. If I opened a bag of potato chips, it was a near guarantee that I would finish the whole thing. I did also eat a lot of fruits and vegetables, but my real saving grace was always running around with friends from the time school ended until I had to be home for dinner and during the summer from early morning until bedtime.

It took many years of education, contemplation and self-reflection to change my eating habits, and to adopt the lifestyle of "eating to live" over my former addiction of "living to eat." I have been a vegetarian now for more than 20 years. It has been and continues to be an amazing learning process for me. Growing up in New York City, I joined in the number one pastime of our family and for most people, which was—and still is— eating. Food was even more accessible to me working in the restaurant industry for many years, waiting tables and bartending. So today, I am writing to you about food. Perhaps the first thing to mention is what the definition of *food* actually is.

Food is a nourishing substance, to sustain life and promote growth. What we eat can have profound affects on the way we think, feel and behave and on society itself. My definition of food may be a little different than most, as I believe it should promote health and not detract from it. That is part of what the word *nourish* means. You can eat lots of things that detract from your health, usually for taste alone. I think that those substances, although edible, should have a different name than *food*. Your body creates an enzyme called *trehalase*, which breaks down the sugar *trehalose* that bugs are partly made of. This is why you are capable of eating and digesting bugs, but I would not call bugs food!

It is very rare now that I eat any animal products at all. I am a vegan who on a rare occasion has a bit of cheese. I try to keep my diet as raw as possible. The times that I have kept to a strict, diverse raw vegan diet for more than 30 days, I felt super-human. My senses became heightened and it seemed that paranormal activities became almost commonplace. There is no effective way to put this into words. It is simply experiential, and you will have to experience it for yourselves someday.

You three girls have all been vegetarian since you were born. I am so proud that your mother and I have learned enough to nourish you exceedingly well on a plant-based diet. I have every hope to teach you all I know about food and nutrition, and to introduce you to some of my heroes on the frontier of the vegetarian movement.

The man who was my first real hero-author is John Robbins. John's story is amazing as he was the heir to the billion-dollar Baskin-Robbins empire, and he gave it all up to live and teach a healthier way of life through diet. You can read his story for yourselves in his many books, such as *Diet for a New America*, *The Food Revolution* and most recently *The New Good Life: Living Better than Ever in an Age of Less*. I was already a vegetarian when I read *Diet for a New America*, but John validated for me why I was a vegetarian in dozens of ways I had never thought of. That book and *The Food Revolution* are to this day two of the most well-resourced books I have ever come across. I will always be grateful and indebted to John Robbins.

In the picture accompanying the beginning of this letter, I am feeding you girls agave-sweetened, coconut-milk based, vegan "ice cream" called Coconut Bliss. I wish that there were products like that when I was your age. I watched the vegan movement soar through the late 1980s and the 1990s with the invention of every type of product from vegan meats to ice creams, all made from soy. Although healthier than their animal ingredient counterparts, these products were still not very healthy, as they were heavily processed. They did, however, satisfy the emotional needs for many like me who were addicted to animal-based foods. These products were stepping-stones for me and helped bridge the gap between my former and current eating habits.

While living in New York I later discovered vegetarian and vegan restaurants, including Angelica's Kitchen and Candle Café. Nowadays, there are too many in New York to list, but the ones I enjoy the most are Candle 79 and Pure Food and Wine. I also have to mention Lula's Apothecary in New York's Alphabet City, which makes the most incredibly delicious nut milk-based ice creams. My friends cannot tell the difference, although Lula's ice creams have better and more intense flavors than their *cow-nterparts* (Hardy, har har!)

After moving to San Francisco, I discovered restaurants like Greens, Herbivore, Millennium, Cha Ya, Shangri-La, Gracias Madre and Café Gratitude. Chef Eric Tucker at Millennium is one seriously talented chef. I have never taken a meat eater there who wasn't amazed at the food. My favorite New York City restaurant, Candle 79, claims that more than 80 percent of the people who dine there are not vegan or even vegetarian.

The consciousness of the connection between a plant-based diet and health has grown exponentially into the mainstream in just the last decade. My favorite Los Angeles restaurant is Real Food Daily. I frequent the Santa Monica location whenever I can and satisfy all of my emotional needs every time I dine there, especially for brunch. Ann Gentry is the owner whose amazing vision and food have led to an upcoming satellite location that will be the nation's first vegan restaurant at an airport!

After being vegetarian and then vegan for many years, I got turned onto the raw food movement in part by your mother. The movement had been dormant since pre-industrialist times, resurfacing with the book *Metaphysics of Raw Foods* written by Stella McDermott in 1919. Then in 1930, Dr. Paul Kouchakoff at the Institute of Clinical Chemistry in Lausanne, Switzerland, showed us that the body's "normal" toxic reaction to eating, know as *digestive leukocytosis*, occurred only when cooked food was eaten. He found that leukocytosis (the immediate increase in our white blood cell count) did not occur if plant foods were eaten in their natural, unheated state. Leukocytosis is also the stress response found normally when the body is invaded by a dangerous pathogen or trauma. He showed us that we have no stress response when we eat purely raw plant-based foods!

The first modern Western book on the raw vegan diet wasn't published until 1974, when Viktoras Kulvinskas wrote *Survival into the 21st Century*. More books would follow, and now the movement continues to grow through authors and chefs such as Gabriel

Cousens, Chad Sarno, David Wolfe, Angel Ramos, David Jubb, and Juliano Brotman.

Juliano, who is the owner and chef of Planet Raw in Los Angeles, Calif. grew up with a meat-heavy diet, became vegan at 19 and completely raw vegan at 23. He writes in his book *Raw: The Uncook Book*: "Without cooking, my energy grew and my consciousness became more aware of the beautiful earth around me. In search of like-minded individuals, I moved to San Francisco to join an Ayurvedic yoga center. Practitioners of Ayurveda, originally a Hindu medicine system, follow dietary recommendations such as always eating hot food in cold seasons. They said, 'Cooked rice is, like, 5,000 years old," and I said, 'Raw was, like, before fire.' So I moved out of the yoga center and got into the restaurant. I just opened the restaurant to eat."

While dining at Juliano's *Planet Raw*, I once had a raw vegan meal including a mushroom gumbo that was so good it literally changed my life! It changed my consciousness about what was possible and how the limitations of our preconceived notions imprison us in our lives. Thanks Juliano, and thank you to all you wonderful, insightful, pioneering, compassionate human beings who promote an animal-free diet.

Dr. Gabriel Cousens made a documentary titled *Simply Raw: Reversing Diabetes in Thirty Days*. He proves that the results from just changing one's diet can be nothing short of miraculous. This film is a must-see. His books *Conscious Eating, Spiritual Nutrition* and *Rainbow Green Live Food Cuisine* are a testament to the highest ideals of the science, philosophies and spirituality of the raw vegan food movement.

Compassion is another key word we need to discuss when it comes to food. Will Tuttle wrote a great book titled *The World Peace Diet*. In an article from *Vegetarian Voice Magazine*, he is quoted as saying, "By placing humans at the top of the planet's food chain, our culture has historically perpetuated a particular worldview that requires from its members a reduction of essential feelings and awareness, and it is this process of desensitization that we must understand if we are to comprehend the underlying causes of oppression, exploitation and spiritual disconnectedness. When we practice eating for spiritual health and social harmony, we practice making certain essential connections that our culturally induced food rituals normally require us to block from awareness. This practice is an essential prerequisite for evolving to a state of consciousness where peace and freedom are possible."

An animal-free diet allows for a more peaceful society. Will states, "This is actually the dawning of veganism within us, which is, as Donald Watson, who coined the word in 1944 said, the urge to live in such a way as to minimize the cruelty we cause others." Will continues by listing the many ways eating animals contributes to suffering and cruelty, including animals being slaughtered or killed through collateral damage, humans being deprived of grain fed to animals bound for wealthier nations, the emotional distress endured by slaughterhouse workers, the negative effects on our ecosystem and on future generations, and so much more. I highly recommend you read Will's fantastic book—his thoughts really strike home with me.

I think you girls are already on the right track. On a visit to New York, we were eating dinner and your grandmother was enjoying some chicken in addition to our vegetarian items. Jana was 4½ years old and said to her, "Grandma, you eat chicken?" She replied, "Sometimes I do." Then Jana replied, "Oh, poor chicken." Witnessing just how compassionate you girls can be warms my heart.

There are whole bunches of compassionate and brilliant people throughout history who have advocated a vegetarian diet. Einstein, the Dalai Lama, Tolstoy, Gandhi, Da Vinci, Albert Schweitzer, Isaac Bashevis Singer, Plutarch and Pythagoras have all espoused famous quotes about vegetarianism. My favorite is from Pythagoras who will be famous to you from high school geometry class. None of my math teachers ever mentioned this quote to me: "What wickedness to swallow flesh into flesh, to fatten greedy bodies by cramming in dead bodies, to have one living creature fed by the death of another. As long as men continue to be the destroyer of animal life, he will never know health or peace and will kill each other. Indeed he who sows the seed of murder and pain cannot reap joy and love." Pythagoras said those words 2,600 years ago. I hope you will come to agree that he was ahead of his time.

I expect that as you children come of age and want to try new things, the day will come where curiosity, naiveté, peer pressure and rebellious behaviors will get the best of you. You will rationalize to yourselves that you should at least taste these things and make up your own minds. I agree that you should make up your own minds, so if and when the day comes that you want to taste meat, poultry and fish, I will be the first one to take you to the finest restaurants to do so. You should all be blessed with the ability to think for yourselves, the openness to absorb truth rapidly and the willpower to implement those truths into your daily lives.

I am only here to guide you by teaching you what I have learned, offering you my opinions, wisdom and spirituality, and loving you as deeply as possible with all my heart and soul. I will never judge you for the decisions you make in your lives, but I will always hold you responsible for self-reflection and contemplation of those decisions. That is one of my jobs as your father.

Your world will be the one you create for yourself. I hope and pray that after you have grown into your own ideals that this ideal of *eating to live* is one that you dearly embrace. Your body, mind and soul will thank you for it. In my own life for the last 20 years, I have only felt the rewards of my plant-based diet. I never feel like I am missing out on anything except perhaps an excess of fatigue, gloom and disease.

Love you always,
Dad

Energy, Universal Intelligence and Conscious Living

Jana's 1st birthday
San Mateo, Calif.
May 2007

Beyond ideas there is a field. Will you meet me there?

—Rumi

September 2012

Dear girls,

I grew up in a very different world than the world of today. Information was a lot harder to come by. When I was growing up, we had a set of encyclopedias. We had to go to the library to look stuff up. It took more time to learn things, and that dictated and limited the rate of our ability to evolve.

Twenty years ago, I could never have imagined that I would be writing you a letter about energy and consciousness. I had no understanding of these things, just an intuition. In 20 years from now, you will have a greater understanding of things than I could ever have dreamed possible. There is a reason for this. It is called the *accelerating rate of returns*, which states: *The rate of change in evolutionary systems increases exponentially.* Ray Kurzweil first explained this axiom in his 1999 book *The Age of Spiritual Machines*. This time in history is unique. Things are evolving so fast that everyone is talking about the fact that things are evolving so fast. We are on the verge of something. Perhaps it will turn out to be the brave new world we have all been hoping for.

I want to begin by discussing energy. Everything is energy. At the core of your being, you are made of energy. You are connected to everything in the universe through a matrix of energy. You are made of the exact same material as everything else. The differences you see come only from how this energy is expressed.

You are a channel for this energy that is Universal Intelligence. You have the ability to tap into Universal Intelligence because you are already a tiny part of it. Take a cup of ocean water out of the ocean and it is still ocean. Anything you need to know and anything you need to do can be aided by your ability to connect to Universal Intelligence.

There is warmth and a positive expression of energy when you see a sunset, when you look up at the night sky to see the moon and stars, when you see a rainbow after a rainstorm, when you are moved by a piece of music, when you smell the fragrance of flowers, when you hold someone's hand, when you hear someone laugh, when you hear rain on the leaves of the trees, when someone smiles at you and when you feel loved by another. Beyond the warmth, beyond the beauty and beyond how these things affect you on an emotional level, there is something deeper.

If you search deep inside you will realize that there is recognition. The word re-cognition is defined as "the identification of something as having been previously seen, heard or known." Your familiarity to existence itself and your ability to recognize is due to your sameness and your communion with all other things. That familiarity you feel to all that exists is because you literally are the sunset, you are the fragrance of the flowers, you are the rainbow, you are the smile and you are the love. All of it is energy.

Your ability to effectively tap into this infinite energetic wisdom is based upon your every thought and action, and the way you live your life. You are like a funnel that allows the universe to flow energy through your brain to be transmutated into thought forms and eventually be put into action. In his wonderful book *Power Thinking*, E. H. Shattock states "aspiration, faith, confidence and conviction are the attitudes of mind that will indicate the extent to which it is possible to clear a path for the transmission of mind-directed energy."

Your state of mind will also dictate the state of your body. The Yoga master B.K.S. Iyengar was quoted as saying, "The body is your *temple*. Keep it pure and clean for the *soul* to reside in." Every choice you make will have an effect on your energetic state. Every thought, every meal, every action will affect the potential and the balance of your energetic state.

All mental and physical things have an energetic or vibrational frequency. Your thoughts, your food, flowers, your body, the earth, the sun and the celestial bodies all have a vibrational frequency. This vibration is palpable if you put your full attention on it. If you take a few minutes to sit down with a flower or plant and truly give it all of your attention, you will be able to feel its energy. With practice you will be able to feel yourself entering into a state of communion with it.

With enough practice, this communion expands, so that one eventually feels connected to the fabric of existence itself. The Hindu expression *Sat-Chit-Ananda* refers to this communion with all of existence or the energetic state of non-duality. Sri Chinmoy, as well as many other enlightened beings, has shared the wisdom that Sat is divine Existence, Chit is divine Consciousness, and Ananda is divine Bliss. When we go deep within, we feel these three together, and when we acquire the inner vision to perceive them all at once and as the same, we live in the Kingdom of Heaven.

Energy is linked to consciousness and plays a cardinal role in healing, health and vitality. It is scientific fact that thoughts can manifest as diseases in the body. Just the results of the placebo effect alone should be enough to convince the greatest skeptic. Belief is powerful medicine. All diseases that manifest in the physical body have their origins in the conscious or subconscious mind. They are the effects of your thoughts and feelings. The documentary *The Placebo Effect* along with the books *Love, Medicine, and Miracles* by Dr. Bernie Siegel, *Breaking the Habit of Being Yourself* by Dr. Joe Dispenza, and the previously mentioned *The Biology of Belief* by Dr. Bruce Lipton and *The Hidden Messages in Water* by Dr. Masaru Emoto are some of the great current resources for affirmation of this subject.

When it comes to the physical health and vitality of the body, energy can be categorized as being energy positive, energy negative or energy neutral. This can be interpreted as how something adds to or detracts from the net overall energy of the body and mind. A half hour spent in meditation will be energy positive while the same half hour spent in worry will be energy negative. An apple and a handful of almonds will give an overall greater positive net energy to the body than will a Big Mac. Decisions made with purpose and in consideration of one's energetic state as a priority leads to conscious living.

Conscious living is a type of discipline or spiritual practice. The discipline to control your thoughts will lead to the discipline to control your feelings, leading to the discipline to control and direct your actions. This type of discipline leads to energy efficiency or "right action." When you feel the communion with Universal Intelligence and you have achieved this type of discipline of mind, you will typically direct your actions and your life's purpose toward the benefit of all, instead of just the benefit of the little you.

The discipline of conscious living and all spiritual practices are evolutionary and the benefits are seen over time. I have been meditating now for close to 18 years and although I felt benefits after a month or two, I realize that the process and the practice take time for one to approach the full potential of what meditation has to offer.

I have been exercising for 30 years, and after many methods of trial and error I feel like I have finally created some efficiency. After my childhood indoctrination of overeating and later decades of gluttony even as a vegetarian, I finally feel like I have a grip on the emotionality that caused my need to overeat. After 30 years of receiving chiropractic adjustments, I can look back on my process of healing, of being virtually drug free, and the clarity of my mind and resilience of my body that have come along with keeping my nerve system free of harmful interference. (I purposefully don't use the term *nervous system*, and if you're wondering why, it's because a mentor, Reggie Gold, would often use the term *nerve system* when referring to the nervous system in his lectures. "It's a system of nerves," he'd say. "So when did it become 'nervous?'" I had to train myself to say *nerve system* instead of *nervous system*, but now I see that the distinction is relevant, and it comes naturally.)

Conscious living requires constant self-evaluation, which leads to efficiency, clarity and the need to follow the highest vision that you hold in your heart and mind. Conscious living is how you direct your energy toward your divine purpose. Allow yourself your own process in pursuing excellence but with the compassion for your own humanity. Perfection is not realistic. Strive for excellence and know you will make mistakes along the way. Be at peace with your decisions and your indulgences. That is part of what conscious living is all about.

With clarity, you will be able to easily feel the energy that surrounds you. Recently in a hotel room, Jana took the Bible out of the nightstand drawer not knowing consciously what it was. She said to me, "Daddy, when I hold this book in my hands, I am holding the whole world!"

Now, where did that come from? She did not even know what a Bible was. It was just another book to her, but perhaps she could feel the collective energy of those with love and reverence for the Bible worldwide. With clarity comes an amazing ability centered in empathy and kindness. Children often make statements or perform actions that amaze adults. How are children able to have such abilities? It is possible because they are less removed from Universal Intelligence and more able to tap into it.

William Blake said, "Energy is eternal delight..." That is what you are. And that is what everything is. Direct your energy with care and your life will be full of grace and purpose. Feel the energy burning in your belly. Feel the energy opening your heart. Feel the energy guiding your soul.

I leave you with a favorite poem by Tennyson:

> ...Come, my friends,
> `Tis not too late to seek a newer world...
> for my purpose holds
> To sail beyond the sunset,...and tho'
> We are not now that strength which in old days

Moved earth and heaven, that which we are, we are;
One equal temper of heroic hearts,
Made weak by time and fate, but strong in will
To strive, to seek, to find, and not to yield.

Love always,
All-ways,
Dad

Naia and Ananda
Burlingame Calif.
April 2008

Sleep with the Winds

Jana
Riverdale, Bronx, N.Y.
December 2011

Sleep with the winds sweet princess,
Trusty steed at your side,
Deep slumber awaits you,
And the world in your mind.

Create your dreams from the stars,
Mold them in your heart,
Keep God's grace around you,
And your fire burning bright.

No evil can harm you,
You're a sunset on the sea.
Live your life with passion,
To set your spirit free.

—Adam Kleinberg

Chiropractic and the Infinite Innate Intelligence Inside YOU!

Jana, age 3
Santa Cruz, Calif.
September 2009

For thousands of years, professions that ministered to the sick disregarded the inside force (Innate Intelligence), and searched the heavens and earth in a vain attempt to externally find the cause of disease.

—B. J. Palmer

January 2012

Dear girls,

When your mother was giving birth to the twins, Naia, the first to arrive, was having a hard time getting through. Although there was no need for emergency action at the time, our midwife eased things and helped the process along by gently and slightly turning Naia's head manually. This was all the intervention necessary in your twin birth process. However, the repeated compression of contractions, along with even a gentle twisting of Naia's head, was enough to cause a misalignment of her spine, specifically the first top cervical vertebra in the neck called the *Atlas,* which articulates with and supports the skull.

When we arrived at the hospital, I was exhausted. I had been awake about 32 hours by then, but all I could think about was adjusting our newborn twins. A few hours later, after you were placed in incubators, I had a chance. I adjusted Naia by applying a very minor amount of force with my left pinky finger to move her Atlas, and felt it shift back into place with a strong popping sound. An audible sound from gently adjusting the neck of an infant with the end of a pinky finger is uncommon, unless the vertebra is quite misaligned. Sometimes it is hard to understand how such a small and simple thing can make such a profound difference. I can honestly say that Naia's first adjustment may have saved her very life.

Although most infants get through the birth process without obvious injury, most have upper cervical alignment concerns. If these are not corrected, the baby's nerve system, immune system and organ functions will be continually impaired, creating ongoing health problems that can confuse both parents and pediatricians.

A *subluxation* (misalignment) of the Atlas can negatively influence billions of nerve fibers. If the Atlas is badly subluxated, the effect can be devastating. Such devastation was revealed in a fascinating research paper. Coroners took X-rays of 74 deceased infants in a specially designed structure that put their spines through a range of motion. In this triple-blind study, a dangerous distortion of the Atlas was found in the majority of those infants who had died from SIDS (Sudden Infant Death Syndrome).

When the Atlas is out of alignment, it can press on the brain stem. The brain stem controls breathing. If a bone of the spine is pressing on the brainstem, is it so hard to imagine that the baby's breathing could be affected? Sounds pretty simple to me! Other symptoms of Atlas subluxation include headaches, migraines, neck pain, jaw dysfunction, nausea, heartburn, irritable bowl, constipation, chronic fatigue, fibromyalgia, depression, anxiety, hypertension, sleep disorders, ADHD and general immuno-suppression. This list of symptoms caused from subluxation of the Atlas was provided, ironically, by the website of a medical doctor. Most medical doctors don't understand the power of chiropractic that allows optimal healing to occur.

How many parents are aware of this simple fact? How many parents have the spines of their newborns checked after birth? Chiropractic has been one of the very greatest gifts in my life. I shudder to think about the health problems that Naia's little Atlas could have caused if it had been left uncorrected.

The lack of understanding of this vital health concern can then lead to children being poisoned with unnecessary medications and chemotherapy, cut open for unnecessary surgeries, and burned with unnecessary radiation due to parents or guardians that are misinformed and misguided. How many children are suffering in the world due to something that could possibly be corrected in a good chiropractor's office? I hope this is painting a different picture of chiropractic than the one most people are used to seeing. Frank Zappa said, "The mind is like a parachute, it works best when it is open."

My own experience attests to this. When I was 6 years old, I had such a painful earache that I was in agony. No medication that the medical doctors at the clinic gave me was working. I just sat there and cried. As a result, they convinced my mother to sign a waiver so the doctors could give me morphine. That was their answer, to give a 6 year-old child morphine for an earache!

There is a small muscle called the *levator veli palatini* in the middle ear that is partly responsible for opening and closing the tube that allows accumulated fluid to drain out of the ear. If the nerve that controls that muscle has pressure on it from a vertebra, that muscle can spasm and the fluid from the middle ear cannot drain properly. This then allows for an environment ripe to breed infection, and pressure builds up and causes the pain.

When the pressure on the nerve is relieved by chiropractic adjustments, the muscle is relieved of spasm, the fluid can drain, and the underlying cause of the problem is gone. This seems pretty logical to me. I wonder how many visits to the specialists and how many poisonous drugs I could have avoided over my childhood years if someone had educated my mother properly!

Well, no one did give Judy the story I am giving you today. The result was that I grew up as one of those kids wearing nose and ear plugs at the swimming pool all summer long to avoid getting horrible earaches. Until I was about 18, I was on a cocktail of several drugs every spring and summer to battle allergies and the mucus that accompanies allergic reactions. Back then, I never would have thought that chiropractic care and later changes in my diet would play such a big part in changing all that.

My chiropractic story begins when at 9 years old I fell from a hammock after the hook suddenly broke on one side. My younger brother and cousin were on top of me, and we had been horsing around. When we fell, I landed on my sacrum, the triangular bone at the base of the spine. Like many undiagnosed common childhood injuries, it hurt for a few days and then went away.

Five years later at age 14, I couldn't figure out why just getting out of bed one day caused me so much pain and made my back decide it didn't want to work right anymore. Thank the stars that my aunt Joyce took me to her chiropractor to be evaluated. That was nearly 30 years ago. I hope she knows what a special gift she gave me that day. Dr. Mitch "fixed" me up pretty good in a few short weeks. I saw Dr. Mitch regularly over the next 12 years.

There were a few times during that 12-year period that I had briefly tried to discontinue my care from Dr. Mitch, but when I did the pain would inevitably return. When I was 23, I moved from New York City to Los Angeles, and I did not see him. Although I had been seeing Dr. Mitch for about nine years then, I disgracefully was never taught that chiropractic adjustments work based on clearing interference from the nerve system. It took me many years to figure out on my own that the process of degeneration takes time before any symptoms are felt.

While living in Los Angeles, I neglected finding a new chiropractor. I didn't fully understand that even though I hadn't been in pain for years, this weakness in my spine required maintenance to not get worse again. I went about six months without getting adjusted, but then the problem resurfaced with a terrible low back pain that crippled me while I was simply walking across my living room floor. I quickly found Dr. Howie in Los Angeles who was a family friend. He "fixed" me up in a few weeks time, once again with no real education about what he was doing.

When I look back, it is so sad to me that these two very capable Doctors of Chiropractic, who I am incredibly grateful to, never took the time to educate me properly. A little passion goes a long way when you are trying to teach. So to set the record straight, chiropractic is a method of keeping the nerve system as clear as possible from interference. A chiropractic adjustment is a transfer of an energetic force by hand into the spine. The body's Innate Intelligence, which is your inborn infinite wisdom, then harnesses that force and distributes it in the most necessary way toward optimal survival or optimal life expression. Pain diminishes when it is no longer needed to protect you from hurting yourself or no longer needs to be a reminder to you that something is wrong and you need to change your habits.

It took several more years until I found myself in chiropractic university, and I began to understand my process, and the inherent philosophies of chiropractic and of Innate Intelligence. I eventually found myself at amazing seminars with people and mentors who were incredibly passionate about chiropractic, health and life itself. I even met your mother in Toronto at a chiropractic seminar called Dynamic Essentials. If it weren't for chiropractic, you three precious girls would not be in my life right now!

Just like every other part of your body, your spine needs maintenance. Unless you put some energy into a system, it will eventually degenerate. Watch what happens if you don't brush your teeth, wash your face or maintain your car. Then after years of breakdown people think, *Gee, I just bent over to pick up the baby and threw my back out.* That would be like saying *Gee, the heart attack I had late last night must be from the Big Mac I had earlier at dinner.*

Many people may not have an understanding of the Innate Intelligence that is within them and how it is always a constructive force. *Innate is always on the job.* Your Innate Intelligence ceaselessly directs the energy within you in the most constructive way possible through your nerve system for every second of your entire life. There is a divine force at work within the body that comes from above-down-inside-out or ADIO. Dr. Timothy Leary, who was certainly not a chiropractor, had a great understanding of this and so entitled one of my favorite books that he wrote, *Your Brain is God.*

I originally wanted to title this letter to you girls "How to Optimize Cellular Regeneration and the Function of Your Central Nerve System," but it sounded too much like the title of a chapter in a textbook. Still, let's look at what an amazing organ your brain is and how it optimally regenerates every cell in your body.

Your brain actually grows you. You actually create yourself. Don't believe me? Cut the nerves that go to your liver and watch your liver wither away. Then tell me what you think. The brain is responsible for growing the entire body, cell by cell. It continues to create and regenerate the body, cell by cell until death. One million cells die and are replaced in the body every second.

A fact commonly recognized scientifically, and according to agedefyingbody.com, your brain recreates a new stomach lining every five days, a new skeleton every 90 days, and a new set of red blood cells every 120 days. A clear nerve system between the brain and the body allows the body to experience this process of optimal cellular regeneration on a moment-to-moment basis. Clearing the nerve system is one of the great gifts of chiropractic to humanity, offering everyone a true fountain of youth.

Innate is always on the job, always. During Naia and Ananda's birth process, the inborn wisdom of the body took over. Ananda was breech with the cord twice wrapped around her neck. You girls were born three weeks early because your Innate Intelligence was aware that if more growth occurred inside the womb, it would have been a detriment to your survival.

In addition to that miracle, during the labor, an intrauterine blood transfer took place. Naia "innately" transferred about 5 percent of her blood to Ananda to give her the additional oxygen she was not getting due to the cord being wrapped around her neck. How did Naia "know" that Ananda needed the blood? Innate Intelligence. Since identical twins share one placenta, the blood transfer from one twin to the other may have made the difference between life and death. We discover and can recognize the infinite Innate Intelligence we have within us when we are witness to these miracles with open eyes, open minds and open hearts.

The history of chiropractic is full of miraculous events. The first modern-day chiropractic adjustment by D.D. Palmer in 1895 helped a man named Harvey Lillard get his hearing back. The second helped a man with a heart problem. Chiropractic is documented as effective against polio. How then, did chiropractic as a profession, go from those amazing beginnings to its current state, where the focus of the majority of practitioners is primarily on treating back pain, neck pain and headaches?

I have witnessed people getting well from just about every sickness and malady known to man through chiropractic care. I try to not take these occurrences for granted, and I also try my best to help other people understand how this type of healing is possible. The world is very sick right now, and a small number of chiropractors who see the light are the keepers of a sacred trust. If children were adjusted instead of drugged from the beginning of their lives, wouldn't we have a healthier world right now?

Many of the world's best athletes utilize chiropractic care for performance. Jerry Rice is the main spokesperson for the Foundation for Chiropractic Progress, and credits the longevity of his career in large part to chiropractic care. He along with Joe Montana, Tiger Woods, Martina Navratilova, Emmitt Smith, Lance Armstrong, John Stockton, Evander Holyfield and David Beckham all use a chiropractor.

Tennis superstar Martina Navratilova stated in a column she wrote for the magazine *Natural Health*, "A chiropractor was instrumental in putting my body back together. Since then I've visited the chiropractor many times for a variety of problems and solutions. As Americans become more aware of the need for preventive medicine, alternative therapies will play a bigger role in our lives. After all, people like what works."

It has not always been this way. The chiropractic profession was persecuted from its origin. The American Medical Association was found guilty by the Supreme Court in Wilk vs. the AMA of conspiracy against the chiropractic profession. Throughout the Wilk case the chiropractors' evidence that included official AMA memos showed the waging of a systematic campaign to destroy the credibility of any alternative health care field. Because chiropractic was the most threatening to them, it was their prime target.

Distorted information and outright lies were spread about chiropractic, which the AMA labeled as an "unscientific cult." Doctors were forbidden to refer patients to chiropractors or accept referrals from them. Doctors of chiropractic were barred from working in hospitals or from even ordering diagnostic tests from medical facilities.

Things have changed since then, but the majority of chiropractors still base their treatment on an outdated, pain-based model. Most of the chiropractic schools have lost their way and are turning out chiropractors that do not have a solid understanding and philosophy about their own profession. On my first day of chiropractic school, our president asked our class of 48 students how many had ever been adjusted by a chiropractor. Only about 12 hands went up. I was mortified. I thought to myself, *What are you people doing here when you have no idea what this is actually all about?*

B. J. Palmer said, "You never know how far reaching something you think, say or do today will affect the lives of millions tomorrow." I often wonder where I would be without chiropractic care. I would likely have been poisoned perpetually with drugs and eventually cut open for unnecessary surgery. That sequence of events has become too commonly a sad story for too many people in recent years.

I also wonder how different you girls would be without the power of chiropractic in your lives. You are all very happy and healthy girls. I know in my heart that the chiropractic care I have given you has made a crucial difference to your health. Even before you were born, your mother was getting adjusted by me not only for her own health and comfort, but also to make sure that you unborn children would blossom full-flowered.

The mother's brain supplies the power to grow the baby inside the womb, cell by cell by cell. Doesn't it then make sense that the pathway between the brain and the growing baby should be kept unobstructed for the baby's optimal development? When you are pregnant, forget about playing Mozart on your belly—it has been proven not to work. But do make sure to go get adjusted because chiropractic does!

I have now had chiropractic care in my life for 30 years, and I can say confidently that it has never failed me, ever. I have seen incredible things in the 16 years since I began my professional education. In my 12 years in practice, I have always educated my patients to the best of my ability with a mandatory presentation. I believe that education is the most important part of helping people. The word *doctor* means "teacher," (from the Latin root, *docere*), and any doctor who cares about people realizes that what doctors do is teach people to make wiser choices regarding their health and wellness. This requires education. An old Chinese proverb states, *Give a man a fish, and you feed him for a day. Teach that man to fish, and you feed him for a lifetime.*

Chiropractic also complements my other philosophies in life and augments the synergy of all my lifestyle practices. I exercise, digest food, meditate, work and express myself more efficiently when my nerve system is working optimally. I express my inner being more fully when my nerve system is clear. The nerve system controls everything, so doesn't that just make logical sense?

You three girls have been adjusted regularly since you were born. Other than one time when you were battling a nasty pneumonia, you have never taken any pharmaceutical drugs. None of you have ever been vaccinated for anything, nor will you ever be while I am alive. It is encouraging to see the growing number of people who are educating themselves to see the scam of the multi billion-dollar vaccine business.

Americans are leading the way in allowing themselves to be brainwashed by pharmaceutical companies and the many pawns they manipulate called doctors. We are only 4 percent of the world population and yet we consume 50 percent of all drugs! The main false belief is that a drug can return health to the body. How could a drug that, if taken by a healthy person will make him sick, ever make a sick person healthy? The problem is the common view of what health is. Health is not an absence of symptoms! People die from heart attacks every day with a complete lack of symptoms. Does that mean they were healthy the day before?

The word *subluxation* is commonly understood to mean a spinal misalignment. Its Latin root, though, means "in the state of less light." A great chiropractor named Thom Gelardi, who is the founder and the former president of the Sherman College of Straight Chiropractic, stated in an interview that, "vertebral subluxation reduces one's creative potential, expression of virtue, and appreciation of beauty, all of which enhance life." This statement is a small sample of the spiritual nature of chiropractic care. Creative potential, expression of virtue and appreciation of beauty may not fit into a triple blind clinical outcome study, but it is a logical conclusion that if a person has interference in the nerve system, then that person will have a diminished capacity in all ways.

I am so very proud to be a chiropractor. I am proud to be part of a legacy that fights against the tyranny of evil men. I am proud to be part of a legacy of enlightenment in the realm of health, healing, wellness and wholeness. I am proud to be part of a healing art that, in its true foundations, welcomes a more complete view of science and gives validity to not only the physical but to the spiritual as well.

The founding fathers of chiropractic, D. D. Palmer and his son B. J. Palmer, wrote great volumes of work on the science, philosophy, art and spirituality underlying this simple and profound healing art. These volumes are known simply as the Green Books. A very popular one that is dear to the hearts of many principled chiropractors is by B. J. Palmer and is appropriately titled *The Bigness of the Fellow Within* in reference to our infinite Innate Intelligence.

I will continue to adjust you girls to make sure all three of you reach your optimal health and creative potential through the gift of chiropractic. You are all so good about climbing up on my chiropractic table for your adjustments, and we typically laugh together through the entire process. I know that chiropractic adjustments are one of the most important ways I can contribute to your well being, and I look forward to the miracles we will see with the help of chiropractic, as you meet your life's inevitable physical, emotional and spiritual challenges.

I sometimes ponder just how many lives I have touched and consequently how many lives chiropractic has touched. We need to keep changing the world one spine at a time. Ben Harper wrote a song that became an instant chiropractic anthem. I don't think he had any idea he was doing that when he wrote the song "My Own Two Hands"

Ben sings about making the world a better and kinder place with your own two hands.

Always remember when you have lost your patience or equanimity, when you are just not feeling right, or when you are feeling disconnected and you can't exactly put your finger on it, that the answer is potentially just an adjustment away. I feel so blessed to be your teacher. I feel so blessed to be your chiropractor. I feel so overwhelmingly blessed to be your father.

Love always,
Always
Dad

Naia
Riverdale, the Bronx, N.Y.
August 2011

Part IV
Success

Jana
Burlingame, Calif.
May 2008

How to Succeed at *Anything*!

Naia and Ananda
Riverdale, the Bronx, N.Y.
July 2011

You can have anything you want if you want it desperately enough. You must want it with an inner exuberance that erupts through the skin and joins the energy that created the world.

—Sheilah Graham, author, actress and
nationally syndicated gossip columnist
during Hollywood's Golden Age

January 2012

Dear girls,

Wow, "How to succeed at *anything!*" I wish someone had written this letter to me 35 years ago!

Recently, I read two books that I found very inspirational: *Power Thinking* by E.H. Shattock and *The Four Agreements* by Don Miguel Ruiz. I reasoned that combining the universal principles contained in the two books would help one to achieve not only success, but would also allow for joy and grace through the process.

In *Power Thinking,* E. H. Shattock writes, "It is fortunate that, in order to develop the power that lies latent in the mind, we require vision, determination, patience, faith in the outcome of our efforts, and, above all, time. It is fortunate because during this time we have the opportunity and will feel the compulsion to develop our higher qualities…"

Vision is the ability to see clearly what you want to manifest into the world. The more clearly you can see something and define it in your mind, the more likely it is that it will come to be. You should be able to see it as if it already exists. You need to define your vision in as many ways as you can. Be detailed! Write it all down! Statistics show that only 2 percent of Americans actually write down their goals but also show that people who write down their goals have more than an 80 percent higher success rate of achieving them! Make sure your goals are clearly written along with the plans to accomplish them.

Don't delay in writing down your thoughts of inspiration because thoughts can be fleeting. Ideas that come to you seemingly from thin air, especially ones that benefit others, are catalysts for your personal growth as a human being. Do not ignore these thoughts but rather embrace them and trust your intuition. When the right ideas come to you, they will have a passion attached to them. You will feel that passion deeply, it will resonate with your entire being, and your passionate vision will lead you to develop determination.

Determination is defined as a firmness of purpose or a resolve, a fixed intention or resolution. I love this quote by Paul Graham from his book *The Anatomy of Determination*:

> *Talent is overrated, compared to determination. Determination implies your willfulness is balanced by discipline. Most people don't know how ambitious to be, especially when they're young. They don't know what's hard, or what they're capable of and this problem is exacerbated by having few peers. Ambitious people are rare, so if everyone is mixed together randomly, as they tend to be early in people's lives, then the ambitious ones won't have many ambitious peers. When you take people like this and put them together with other ambitious people, they bloom like dying plants given water. Probably most ambitious people are starved for the sort of encouragement they'd get from ambitious peers, whatever their age. Achievements also tend to increase your ambition. With each step you gain confidence to stretch further next time.*

The more committed you are to making something happen, the more likely that it will. Determination has to do with your willpower. People make all kinds of excuses every day for giving up, such as, *It was too hard, I was sick, my boyfriend broke up with me, I just got divorced, I was in an earthquake, my cousin died, I didn't make the team, I got fired, I have no money, I couldn't find the time, I have two kids.* These and many other excuses keep most people from fulfilling their destiny, from reaching toward their higher potential.

Determination has no excuses. Determination requires commitment. Determination will lead you through tears and hardship like a ship determined to get through a terrible storm. Your passionate vision along with your determination will lead you to develop patience.

Patience is defined as tolerant and even-tempered perseverance. It takes great discipline to be tolerant and even-tempered while persevering through the trials and tribulations of life. Although your fire and passion of vision and determination want it all to happen now, you must develop a certain non-attachment to the outcome in order to cultivate patience. This is in great part accomplished by mastering the control of your emotions. That, however, does not mean stifling your emotions, so that on the outside you seem calm while on the inside there is turmoil. Mastering control of your emotions comes in great part by directing and streamlining your thoughts. Choosing your thoughts allows you to be steadfast in respect to moving forward toward your goal and keeping your emotions in check.

Rarely do things go according to plan. Of course, a clear vision helps things move along well, but sometimes it is difficult to account for and calculate everything along the path. A synonym for patience is *long-suffering*. My personal belief is that you don't have to suffer if you have developed the discipline of non-attachment. This does not mean that you don't do everything in your power to help your cause. It does mean that if you hit a few road-bumps along the way, you have the discipline to remain tolerant and even-tempered. *If at first you don't succeed, try, try again!* goes the famous slogan. As you move unwaveringly toward your goal, and you start to develop patience, the combination of your passionate vision and determination along with patience will help you to cultivate faith in the outcome of your efforts.

Faith is defined as a strong or unshakeable belief in something especially without proof or evidence. Faith also includes loyalty and devotion to one's own intentions. Faith in the outcome of your efforts is, again, the product of the mastery over your thoughts. It is the ability to set aside doubt and fear, to joyously accept your path, and to know that in time the goal will be accomplished. Faith has a lot to do with how intense your vision is, along with the depth of your commitment. You will develop a deep faith in the outcome of your efforts if your vision is clear, if you are driven by your inner determination, and if you have developed the patience to get through the adversity that comes along with accomplishing anything worthwhile and beneficent.

Faith is also about trusting yourself. Inside of you there is an infinite, inborn wisdom that you and all people possess. No one needed to teach you as a newborn how to see with your eyes or to suckle a breast. Look within to this infinite Innate Intelligence to be your guide. Stay conscious of the universal energy that connects everything. It will give you the strength and guidance to achieve whatever you want. Knowing that your efforts are worthwhile, regardless of the outcome should be incorporated into your faith.

B. J. Palmer, one of the founding fathers of the chiropractic profession said, "You never know how far-reaching something you think, say, or do today will affect the lives of millions tomorrow. It is better to light one candle than to curse the darkness. Get the big idea and all else follows." Although you may never reach your goal, you may touch many people with your love and devotion along the way. You may plant a seed. Be the unwavering inspiration that people are so in need of in this world. You can be that inspiration if you have faith in yourself and in the outcome of your efforts.

Vision, determination, patience and faith are the tools, but they require time in order for you to bring your goal to fruition.

Time is a construct of your mind. Time is also relative. Einstein explained relativity in this famous quote, "Put your hand on a hot stove for a minute, and it seems like an hour. Sit with a pretty girl for an hour, and it seems like a minute. That's relativity." You can bend time with your mind. Vision, determination, patience and faith will allow you to bend time, like Super Girl bending a thick metal rod as if it were a paper clip.

Allow yourself a truly sufficient amount of time to achieve your goal. Know that there will be difficulties along the way, even if you cannot see the root of the challenges that might present themselves. Account for those challenges. When you have attachment to the outcome happening in a specific amount of time, pressure mounts, and time becomes your enemy. Anxiety, worry, pressure and frenetic energies come from a lack of thought discipline. When you are not attached to the outcome and you are enjoying the process inclusive of the easy parts and the challenges, time will be your friend. We feel time pass as a sequence of thoughts in the mind. Discipline over those thoughts, and the freedom from thought altogether that comes as a result of dedication and meditation can allow you to benefit from the relative nature of time.

As time passes, you will realize that when you were young, there were few things of any importance that you got to choose. You did not choose to live in Canada. You will not choose your school, your language, your values and morals, or your spirituality. You will be indoctrinated by many influences in your life. As you get older, it is paramount that you reflect on the origin of the way you see things; your worldview.

The second wonderful and poignant book I recently read is *The Four Agreements* by Don Miguel Ruiz. Ruiz explains that you never get the opportunity to choose what to believe and what not to believe. "We need a great deal of courage to challenge our own beliefs... Ninety-five percent of the beliefs we have stored in our minds are nothing but lies, and we suffer because we believe all those lies... but the most important agreements are the ones you made with yourself."

If you follow Ruiz's Four Agreements in your life, you will not only have the tools to succeed, but you will also have the tools to move toward your goals with integrity and without harming anyone. But the Four Agreements run deeper than goals to bring something about; they are also ways to live consciously without doing harm. They are:

#1. *Be impeccable with your word.* Ruiz writes, "The word is a force; it is the power you have to express and communicate, to think and thereby create the events in your life."

#2. *Don't take anything personally.* This is another way of saying remain unattached to the outcome. I have a best friend who believed that only bad things happened to him. *Why is this happening to me?* was his catchphrase, as if the universe were delivering negativity to him personally.

#3. *Don't make assumptions.* Assumptions are fears about things you are making up in your mind. Your mind can take you on a roller coaster ride to invent a fictitious future with consequences you are not very fond of. This can make you feel like a hamster trapped on a running wheel. Keep calm in your mind and be patient to make sure you have all the facts before you allow yourself to react prematurely.

#4. *Always do your best.* This may sound obvious. Your best will always vary, but you will know if you search your heart and are honest with yourself, if you really gave it your all.

I believe success also comes from living in a state of abundance. You may not have two nickels to rub together, but you may have an overflowing amount of love and kindness to give to others. You may have great wisdom to share with others. The spiritual teacher Sri Chinmoy is quoted as saying, "Just one smile immensely increases the beauty of the Universe." Your abundance and intentions of loving-kindness can shine right through your smile. You can change someone's life with just a smile. People can feel your abundance, and you become a force of attraction.

If you ask people if they want to be happy, they will logically say yes to that question. But ask them what they *do* to be happy, and you might get some blank stares. If you do something you love to do, you will never work a day in your life. Gandhi's famous quote, "Be the change you want to see in the world" is appropriate here.

Success is a state of mind. It cannot be measured by how big your house is or the car you drive. You girls will each measure your success in your own way. Devoting your time to something you believe in with all your passion is already success. Feeling abundance and joy from within is also success. Whatever success you strive for, let it be the success that you design for yourself.

Each of you will eventually find your paths. I hope I have the opportunity to be there for every step along the way.

Love always,
Dad

Jana
Burlingame, Calif.
September 2008

Talkin' 'Bout My Education

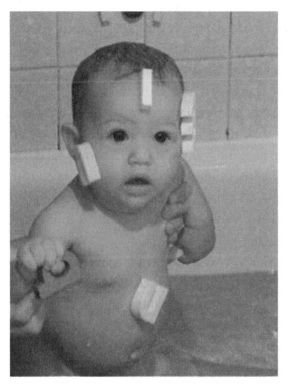

Jana
San Mateo, Calif.
July 2007

Don't think, feel!
It is like a finger pointing away to the moon.
Don't concentrate on the finger, or you will miss all that heavenly
glory!

—Bruce Lee

February 2012

Dear girls,
From a very young age, I was a performer, and for as long as I can

remember, I enjoyed entertaining people and making them laugh. In sixth grade, I played Nanki Poo, the male lead in *The Mikado*. This was my grade school's production of Gilbert and Sullivan's famous operetta set in feudal Japan. It was so much fun! The creative aspect of performing piqued my interest because academics always came very easily to me and often left me feeling bored.

From first grade on at P.S. 96 in the Bronx I was constantly correcting my teachers, especially their math. I was more interested in socializing and making my friends laugh than in what the teacher had to say, or how she wanted us to conform to the behavior that is expected of little girls and boys. Let's face it; conventional schooling is not very fun. We kids spiced it up any way we could, passing notes, shooting spitballs, and we became experts at hiding gum and candy under our tongues.

In third grade, my teacher Mrs. Sender was fed up with the fact that I would not stop talking in class while she was giving her lessons. Our class was set up with the students' desks in the shape of a U and the teacher's desk facing us from the front. Within a couple of months, Mrs. Sender placed my desk 10 feet behind the back row of the class in order to isolate me. I spent the rest of the school year relegated to a back-of-the-room solitary confinement, but the plan backfired on my teacher. Because I was on my own, I stood out even more and became the center of attention with whatever antics I was up to each day. She thought she could break me. She was wrong. It's just a good thing kids weren't commonly being prescribed Ritalin or other behavioral drugs back then. Like the many teachers today who recommend children take toxic and dangerous drugs for behavioral issues, I am sure my teacher would have considered me a prime candidate, just to shut me up!

I share the growing opinion that it is this type of conditioning and conformity that lies at the root of the failure of modern education. In contrast, the spiritual leader Krishnamurti envisioned that education should emphasize the integral cultivation of the mind and the heart, not mere academic intelligence. For decades, he engaged in dialogues with teachers and students, emphasizing the understanding that it is only in the freedom from conditioning that true learning can take place.

As you get older, I am not concerned about you girls learning the basic academics you need in life. I am interested in more than your academic survival. The key to unlock your potential must be a passion that burns within you to acquire knowledge and then wisdom. Wisdom is applied knowledge. It is not enough to know. *To know, and not to do, is not to know*, the expression goes. Learning is a lifelong process. It is my job to be your primary teacher and to oversee the others who are teaching you. It is my job to point you in fruitful directions. I hope to inspire you through leading by example and sharing my passions with you.

I do not believe in most modern conventional education techniques. I don't really care if you miss days at school. As a matter of fact, as you get older, I will take you out of school to spend time with you teaching you about life and taking you on special adventures. On those days, you will learn much more out of school than you would learn in school. We must take advantage of those days properly. You should have your *Ferris Bueller's Day Off* days. Besides, almost any monkey can memorize a bunch of names, numbers and formulas, and spit it back out of its short-term memory. Unfortunately, lots of doctors, lawyers and other professionals get their degrees this way. In many years of education, they sometimes don't learn a damn thing worth remembering.

The world is changing rapidly. The exponential growth of technology is shaping things to change so quickly on a global scale that most people can't keep up. With the totality of human knowledge at the fingertips of the people of developed nations, what is the practical point of memorizing facts, figures and formulas anymore? Is it because outdated teachers want to ensure their students are experts at memorization? Does a future student who is not planning to become a biochemist really need to memorize something like the Krebs cycle? I just don't see the point.

The majority of educational systems are just about broken. They are archaic. Their priorities are confused. There is too much focus on a rigid curriculum and obedience, and opposition to the most important factor that should be the first focus of education: the individual expression of each child. Helping a child toward the expression of her individual potential and talents should sit deep in the heart of the educational system. Teachers need to cultivate the constructive and unique passions of each individual child to develop full-flowered. If this were the case, we would have a more productive society. If this were the case, what a beautiful world it could be.

There are a few forms of education that have a greater credo than most. I am a great admirer of Rudolph Steiner and the Waldorf educational system. In the Waldorf School system, there is a long-term intimate relationship that develops between the teacher and the student. The program calls for the student with the same teacher for multiple years. The student will have the same teacher from the first through the eighth grade and then another teacher from ninth through twelfth grade. The type of relationship that develops with this type of longevity leads to trust, openness and also friendship.

Waldorf also places the artistic expression of the child as one of its highest priorities. The fortification of the imagination and liberation of the creative force of the child can only come through art. Art builds the expression of the individual and allows us to observe our divine nature through creation. This is a process that is hindered by most modern conventional educational systems.

Other priorities of Waldorf are awareness and exposure to multiculturalism. It boasts an academic curriculum that is aligned more accurately to children's psychological development and peak interests. Outside of Waldorf and a few other similar types of educational systems, the constitution of North American education is in need of transformation. Its current configuration is far from a help to the child trying to find their true calling.

I recently watched a documentary film called *Waiting for Superman*. It shows how the educational system is full of long-winded bureaucrats. These foul-smelling politicians prioritize the security of incompetent teachers over the necessary education of the children. It is infuriating to witness the squandering of hundreds of millions and potentially billions of dollars that could go directly to benefit the children. These funds are instead wasted by poor political decisions protecting tenured teachers. It has been this way for many decades, and the system is about to completely collapse into itself.

There is hope, though. It starts with those impassioned, courageous, dedicated and selfless individuals who will let nothing stand in their way to make change. Inside each one of them, the human spirit is on fire with determination to see their dreams of education fulfilled. They won't take no for an answer. These teachers are a *tour de force*, and the results of their dedication have shown to be highly measurable, topping the highest results of education in the world.

What I want to express to you most significantly about your education is that in the end it is up to you. It is your responsibility to read about what interests you. Diligently learn what you need to know, leaving no stone unturned. You should most importantly apply this knowledge into your life through trial and error. Use your time wisely. Read voraciously. Be productive. And remember this always; laziness is your worst enemy.

We have become a society addicted to and mesmerized by materialism, entertainment, celebrity and instant gratification. You will not read Tolstoy overnight. You will not learn to play Debussy's *Claire De Lune* after a few hours of practice on the piano. You will not serve a tennis ball like Stephi Graff after a single lesson. You will not write sonnets like Pablo Neruda after your first introduction to poetry.

Rome was not built in a day. The amount of energy you channel into educating yourself and applying yourself will shine through in the inevitable abilities brought about by your dedication and determination. Ayn Rand, the founder of the philosophy of objectivism and the author of *Atlas Shrugged* and *The Fountainhead* is quoted as saying, "The question isn't who is going to let me; it's who is going to *stop* me?"

Don't let anything get in the way of your self-education; your life will be a direct reflection of the efforts you put forth. I know when the time comes that all three of you girls will make me very proud.

Love always,
Dad

Heaven, Blossom and Bliss

Jana
Kingston Ontario, Canada
June 2010

You are the light,
you are pure love,
you are my gift,
from the stars above.

Jana is Heaven, so lovely and bright.
Naia is Blossom, a seed with great might.
Ananda is Bliss, always laughing aloud.
I can't fathom a father that could be more proud.

When the world seems too cold
And discouragement flares,
Find the courage within
To carry on and still care.

Life's struggles are illusions,
The Bluebirds sing their tune,
Shine your love on the world,
Like flowers in full bloom.

—Adam Kleinberg

Ananda and Naia
Ontario, Canada
June 2010

I Love My Bicycle

Ananda, Naia and Jana
Ontario, Canada
October 2010

When the spirits are low, when the day appears dark, when work becomes monotonous, when hope hardly seems worth having, just mount a bicycle and go out for a spin down the road, without a thought on anything but the ride you are taking.

—Arthur Conan Doyle

February 2012

Dear girls,

The first bike I really loved was an orange, ten-speed Kabuki road bike that my dad had bought me. I added a small blue bag that hung from the back of the seat to hold my things. A few days later, while I was in a store buying a birthday card, my friend Jonathan was outside watching my bicycle. When Jonathan came into the store and asked me what I wanted, I thought it was odd. When he went back outside, the man who told him his friend wanted to see him had stolen my Kabuki. It was only my second ride on it that day.

The thief rode my bicycle east on the service road of Pelham Parkway South from White Plains Road, headed toward Williamsbridge Road. My brother at that very moment happened to be looking out our sixth floor apartment kitchen window. He saw the thief racing down the road and said to himself, *Hey, that guy has the same bicycle as Adam—he even has the same little blue bag!* I would never see my beautiful Kabuki again. I know bicycles get stolen everywhere, but to me this is just another *Bronx Tale.*

A much more famous bicycle ride occurred on April 19, 1943, taken by the Swiss chemist Albert Hoffman who went for a 2-mile ride after ingesting his newest creation, LSD. This day is now known in the psychedelic counter-culture as "bicycle day."

The bicycle is one of the greatest inventions ever. There is nothing that can help you recapture the pure joy and fun of childhood like riding your bike. My first real autonomy and ability to get around quickly as a child was on my bike, and I practically slept with it all through my teen years.

Now as an adult, riding my bicycle helps me keep a slower pace, something more relaxed. It is a way to get places, a way to get exercise, a way to save money and a way to experience motion without any barriers to nature. The wind can blow through your hair, the sun can shine on your face, and you are not a slave to the rules of the road like you are in a car.

There is nothing like riding a bicycle. There is an unparalleled freedom and self-sufficiency that does not exist with any other mode of transportation. Several years of my adult life have been spent without the responsibility or convenience of owning a car. The two cities where I was easily able to ride my bicycle everywhere and anywhere were Amsterdam and Santa Cruz.

Your mother and I lived in Amsterdam for about 15 months, and that is where Jana was conceived in 2005. Amsterdam is flat, small and very easy to get around, so riding a bicycle is the perfect mode of transportation. It rains 300 days a year in Holland, so one always has to have the proper gear to battle off the wind and the rain. If you can stay warm and dry in Amsterdam, there is never a need to complain. With about 1 million people and more than 600,000 bicycles, it is truly the most prevalent bicycle culture in the Western world. I have not been to Shanghai but hear it is equally as impressive.

My two favorite things about being on my bicycle in Amsterdam were riding through the canals on a crisp clear evening and riding through the Vondelpark on a rare sunny day. Never having to find a parking space was an added bonus. After a recent two-month period back in Amsterdam, I was again amazed to see the bicycle culture in action. I saw a pregnant woman with two small children in a specialized family bicycle with groceries hanging on handlebars, riding in the rain! An American woman would never try to live up to the legend of the super-Dutch-bicycle-women. I also was amazed to see a grandmother riding with her two grandchildren sitting on the bicycle while she was walking a dog on its leash at the same time.

When we lived in Santa Cruz, we had two bicycles and two attachments for you three girls. Your mother and I suffered greatly on the hills of the area, especially when riding home from the gym after leg workouts. It was great to go downtown to the farmer's market every week, park our bicycles and enjoy the food, the Santa Cruz sunshine and the familiar beats of the local drum circle. Santa Cruz has a pretty big bicycle culture, but it's nothing like Amsterdam. However, the abundant California sunshine does add to the ease of the bicycle being a primary mode of transportation.

I am looking forward to teaching you girls how to ride your own bicycles. I learned to ride when I was 6 years old while living in Connecticut in 1974. My dad ran with me and sent me on my way down a hill that at age 6 seemed huge but in reality was quite small. The first time I fell, I was taking a 180-degree turn too sharply. Everyone falls in life. You just have to get up, dust yourself off, put on a Band-Aid, wipe off the tears if necessary and get back to your business.

I usually find myself whistling or singing while I ride. Other times I find myself more reflective, paying attention to all the beauty that surrounds me. I try to take as many different routes to the same destination, so I can see different things along the way. In a psychological study done on happiness, the top two life factors for people who consider themselves happy were that they love what they do and that they had a very short commute to their work. A great gift you can give yourself when you are older is setting up your life so you can bike to work. How stress-free it will be for you to take a bike ride to your work every day. You will watch the morning rush-hour traffic going slower in their cars than you riding on your bicycle. I doubt you will be experiencing road rage anytime soon.

Ride your bicycle for the joy of riding. It is certainly an active meditation that will bring you joy and clarity for the rest of your days. Take good care of your bicycle and it will in turn take good care of you. If someday your friend is watching your beloved bicycle for you, tell her not to take her eyes off it, not even for a second. Better yet, just lock it up whenever it is out of your sight. I hope you are spared hearing someone tell you they saw someone riding away on a bike that looked just like yours!

Love always,
Dad

How to Eat a Pink Grapefruit

Naia, Ananda and Jana
Kingston Ontario, Canada
November 2010

Love is a fruit in season at all times, and within the reach of every hand.

—Mother Theresa

October 2011

Dear girls,

For many years, I had no interest in eating grapefruits. I really had no idea how delicious the right grapefruit could be and what I was missing. Fortunately, my girlfriend Lee taught me how to get the most out of eating a pink grapefruit. At first I made fun of her for peeling it because for 25 years, I watched my grandmother cut hers in half and eat section by section with a special serrated spoon. But when I saw how little was left on Lee's plate when she was finished, I knew I had come upon the Great Grapefruit Master. The efficient technique I will describe to you belongs to her.

There is a book titled, *How You Do Anything, Is How You Do Everything.* I find this to be true in most cases. Take care eating your grapefruit with craftiness. The reward is quite yummy-licious! You might get different types of advice on this topic, but look no further, this is the best!

Step 1: Peel the grapefruit. Take care to leave more of the pith (the white part which is the connective tissue) as opposed to exposing the grapefruit segments while peeling. The pith contains all the bitter taste while the segments are sweet and delicious.

Step 2: After peeling, pull the grapefruit into two halves. Take out any center vein from the middle. Begin to pull the pith gently off a single segment, exposing the entire outer side. The pith between segments peels off very easily and cleanly from the vesicles that make up the segments. Now peel down the other side and then separate the bottom of the segment from the pith as well. The segment is then clean of all the pith, its sweetness made available. Now eat and enjoy!

Step 3: Repeat the process. Now you can take the pith off one segment at a time, always peeling back from the crest of the segment. Pull the segment until it separates from the bottom of the pith, and presto, another segment! Continue this until there is nothing left on your plate but the peel and the pith.

It is important to pick a good grapefruit. Try to pick one that feels heavy for its size, usually indicating it will be juicy. It's such a drag to get a grapefruit that looks great on the outside and is dry once you get it open. I prefer a large, organic pink grapefruit. I try to eat fruits primarily when they are in season. When the organic pink grapefruits are in season, they are really big and beautiful. The skin is usually a yellow-orangey-pink with an occasional burst of darker pink.

Although what I've just described is a set of instructions for how to eat a grapefruit, it is also a metaphor for simple guidelines on how to live your life: 1) Have a plan, 2) Be thorough, and 3) Be efficient. It takes brainpower to incorporate these qualities into your life. *Having a plan* comes from anticipating the "what ifs" in life. You should make sure you did all you could in any eventuality. It takes anticipation to prepare for different scenarios, doing your best to leave no stone unturned. *Being thorough* means you are nearly certain or completely certain of the future outcome to the best of your ability. *Being efficient* comes from trial and error. Continue to assess how different things are working for you. Continue to audition different methods that you have thoroughly looked into by committing to them in a disciplined fashion.

And, my three very beautiful daughters, pick your perfect organic pink grapefruit like you would pick a man to share your life with. Examine it closely. Does it meet your standards? Smell it, feel it, commune with it. How does it speak to you? How does it taste? There is a lot to consider if you really think about it. Most importantly, be patient to wait for the right grapefruit and don't just bring any old grapefruit home for me to meet! Wait for a ripe one. Better to wait for a great grapefruit than settle for one that won't change your life and keep you smiling.

And finally, tasting a delicious grapefruit can bring you intensely into the present moment. You will find gratitude behind the pleasure your taste buds signal to your brain. All that *oohing* and *ahhing* over tasting anything delicious when you really analyze it is just an inarticulate attempt at expressing deep spiritual gratitude. Eating a grapefruit can be a spiritual experience. At least it can be if you think of it that way. Eating a grapefruit can be as spiritual as meditating with the Dalai Lama on the top of one of the mountains of the Himalayas. Just being alive affords us so much opportunity to enjoy so many simple, sensual pleasures.

I would like us to have our own grapefruit trees someday. We should love growing, picking and peeling the grapefruits as much as we love eating them. *Love what you are doing when you are doing it.* These are simple words to live by. And take time to enjoy your grapefruit. It's definitely worth it!

Love always,
Dad

Better Safe Than Sorry

Jana
Golden Gate Park Orchid Exhibition, San Francisco, Calif.
March 2010

Wisdom consists of the anticipation of consequences.
—Norman Cousins

Only those who will risk going too far can possibly find out how far it is possible to go.

—T.S. Eliot

November 2010

Dear girls,

When I was 17, your grandmother gave me $3,000 to buy my first car. I chose a pastel yellow 1977 Monte Carlo with a white Landau roof. My twin friends Ira and Stan Ianuzzi immediately tinted the windows for me. I bought it from a used car lot on Boston Road in the Bronx. The salesman saw me coming from a mile away but that car turned out to be a tank and lasted me for several years without too much trouble. After parking on a hill, pushing the gear handle into reverse instead of park and then securing the brake lock, the car started rolling and I crashed through a garage door on East 58th Street in Manhattan. It was the night of my senior prom and we were on our way to a club. I hadn't even had a drink yet.

One night that same year, after work at about one in the morning, my friend Frank invited me and a friend to a party. I knew there would be alcohol there and that there would be girls, too, so I was eager to go. Frank told me follow him there, that it wasn't too far away.

Frank was flying in his car, and I was trying my best to keep up. This was way before cell phones and Google Maps, and I didn't even have the address. I knew if Frank lost me, he wouldn't wait for me to catch up. He passed a wicked curve and clung to the pavement going very fast. The bald tires on my car, unfortunately, did not hold the same traction. I skidded across the double yellow line at the apex of the curve, through two lanes, up onto the sidewalk clear across the street, and hit a fence between a tree and a fire hydrant. If a car had been coming the other way on that busy street, I am pretty sure we all would have been killed. A few days later, Frank called me and asked me why I bailed on him the night in question. He had no idea I had crashed my car, and apparently the party wasn't what it was hyped up to be, after all.

When it comes to life's decision-making processes, there are a few things I hope I can pass on to you girls that will ring alarmingly through your lovely brains before you put your bodies into action. Most important, every decision you make has a consequence. Even the very small decisions you make every day establish the patterns that make up your life. The last-minute decisions you make are usually the ones that are not well thought out and become the ones you wind up regretting the most. You might think, *Gee, I'll only be going into the store for a minute—my bike will be safe without locking it up.* Or, *Oh my God, he is the best kisser—maybe I won't make him wear a condom this time.*

There will be many challenges for you as young women as you go through your major biological changes. The time will come when hormones and impulses seem to take over, and you may feel like you don't even know yourself. You may feel awkward, out of place, like no one understands you. Remember that you will be going through an experience all humans go through. If you have the understanding that your changes are part of a metamorphosis from caterpillar to butterfly, and you also practice patience with yourself, you will suffer less and make your life easier and more productive.

The only way to make smart decisions is to consider the consequences. That doesn't mean you shouldn't take chances in life or occasionally try to beat the odds stacked against you. All the greatest stories are about people who beat the odds, usually with great patience and by sheer determination. The decisions that you make will most importantly be made without fear. Hopefully, there will be practicality in your decision-making, but there should also be times when you make decisions based primarily on your principles and your philosophies, even if the great majority is against you.

Unfortunately, you will encounter great injustice in the world you are about to grow up in. There is an epidemic of scandal and greed, and a general state of apathy among a growing number of nations. There is a great shortage of integrity among the people who are supposed to have your best interests at heart. Please do not take those words to mean that I am a pessimist. I am an eternal optimist with the ability to objectively evaluate and accept what I see around me.

You will make your decisions wisely when you don't give into your emotions. Most of the decisions we make with too much emotion are the ones we also tend to regret soon after. Thoughts like, *I can't believe he dumped me. I am going to get drunk and go crash the party he's at with his new girlfriend* will only get you in trouble.

Decisions like those are made when you are not considering any of the consequences. It is human nature to have thoughts like that, but it's weighing them out for a moment with a clear head and then allowing yourself the acceptance of the situation that will help you make the most constructive decisions.

Choices made out of desperation or deception are the ones that will also come back to haunt you. I hope that as you girls get older, you feel you can talk to me about anything because I will never judge you. Thoughts like, *I really need some money for spring break so maybe I'll go work at that strip club for just a month* will never get you anywhere.

As you grow up, it will be difficult to balance all the thoughts and emotions that may have an effect on your life. Create that one clear moment for yourself and think it out. At the least, you will be proud of yourself that you took the time to try your best and do the right thing, or what seemed like the smartest thing at the time.

Also remember that some of the people closest to you during different phases of your childhood and adolescence, people you consider your friends, will use guilt, lies, begging and bribing to get you to make decisions you don't feel comfortable making. Boys will be especially diligent in this department. There is *nothing* a boy won't do or say to convince you to have sexual relations with him. This is just the truth. When it doesn't feel right to you, it is not right. Always remember that.

Like I did in my little car crash, you will wind up getting away with things and thanking your lucky stars that it turned out the way it did. You will probably also relive the excitement of that moment with friends as you talk about it later on in life, laughing together about the crazy days of your youth. On the other hand, you could wind up suffering dire and potentially deadly consequences. That's just life. That is why it is so important to stop and take just one clear moment to size up any situation before committing to any action.

In a moment, the most fun situation could turn instantly into a nightmare. Just one slip on the roof of the house as you are trying to jump into a pool, one look down to pull your lipstick out of your bag while you are driving over the double yellow line, one unprotected sexual encounter while you may be in a fertile phase or getting into a car for a ride with a bunch of boys you don't really know very well—all of these could leave you in situations with negative conse-quences.

On the other hand, learning to be spontaneous and daring is extremely important if you are going to get the most out of your life. Take calculated and smart risks, and not ones that endanger your life, your safety or the safety of others. Strive after your passions with enthusiasm and determination. Don't be afraid to break the rules because the rules usually suck!

Also, don't be afraid to stand out if that is who you are. There is never anything wrong with being you as long as you don't have intentions of harming others. One way of shining brighter than your peers is by being innovative. Sometimes if you want to be noticed, you have to take matters into your own hands. Try not to let situa-tions keep you from following through on your intuition. The deci-sions you make that allow you to talk yourself out of being brave are the ones you will later regret. We rarely regret the things we do in life, but we often regret the things we didn't even try to do.

Remember that you never have anything to be afraid of. Life is short, and just like all living things, your time will be up before you know it. You will never forget the day that you had a split-second decision to make, and you didn't follow your instinct. As that cute boy rode away on the bus, you looked down at the paper in your hand with your phone number written on it, and you couldn't figure out what had kept you from giving it to him.

Life can turn on a dime. Your life is so precious, and it is also very temporary. It is my job to make sure you make the least amount of poor decisions. I know that you will be let down, hurt, crushed, betrayed, pressured and that you will suffer from many situations life will bring your way. So do yourself a favor. Before you go and tattoo that boy's name on your tush, please think about it first. You just might change your mind.

Love always,
Dad

Reading Is Fundamental

Ananda
Riverdale the Bronx, N.Y.
Christmas 2011

Books are the quietest and most constant of friends;
they are the most accessible and wisest of counselors,
and the most patient of teachers.

—Charles W. Eliot

December 2011

Dear girls,

When I was 13, your grandfather Karl gave me a 1,200-page book titled *Atlas Shrugged* by Ayn Rand. I made it through the first 50 pages. I was a smart kid and although I liked what I could understand of it, I didn't really like to read at that age. I was very active and reading was boring.

It wasn't until my martial arts teacher gave me the same book at age 19 that I was ready to read it. After tearing through the book in three days, I had an intense realization of what my dad wanted for me in life and why he gave that specific book to me at such a young age. The book helped me picture my life as one I could live without compromising my principles or my highest visions. When you read *Atlas Shrugged,* you will know exactly what I am talking about.

In high school, my favorite book was *A Catcher in the Rye* by J.D. Salinger. I think teenagers love this classic book because teens commonly share a lack of confidence and the feeling that they just don't fit in. It is easy to identify with a character like Holden Caulfield, who is considered one of the most important characters of 20th century American literature. I hope that at a young age you girls gain the comfort and insight from this great book that I did, simply to ease the stresses that come along with being a teenager.

It wasn't until I was 20 that I really started using books to learn how to do things and how to do them better. I started reading on my own because I was finally the one who got to pick the books. Anything I wanted to learn, I could learn in a book. The bookstore Barnes and Noble became my favorite hangout. Soon after, I realized that independent used bookstores were the places where I should be spending my money. I could make it last so much longer!

I am still old fashioned about books. I love the way they smell. I love the way they feel. I love their heaviness. I love the artwork of books and their dust covers. I like the way the pages turn and the feel of the page in my hand. A well-constructed book possesses a lot of character, and I do appreciate this.

You can change just about anything in your life or about yourself by reading the right books. You will be given strength, virtuous direction, patience, purpose, faith, self worth, romanticism, creativity, imagination, courage, confirmation, pragmatism, determination, passion and vitality by reading the right books. Mark Twain said, "The man who does not read good books has no advantage over the man who can't read them."

Books will help you to learn more about yourself and your nature. They will illuminate you in ways that you never expected were possible. The only material possessions I am attached to anymore are my books, and that is only so that I can give them to you. Please do not discard them. They are precious to me.

If you read them, they will become precious to you, too. I imagine that as you grow older into this digital age, the inconvenience of non-digital things will feel like a burden, especially 1,500 books, which is the size of my library. Some are rare books. Some are very valuable and will likely continue to increase in value. More than 90 percent are non-fiction. Most importantly, they are a collection.

There are books by pioneers in philosophy, psychology, wisdom traditions, health and wellness, chiropractic, meditation, diet, fitness, yoga, quantum physics, biology, plants, drugs, love, children, naturalism and more. Some of the books on Hinduism, Buddhism, Vedanta and Taoism are the ones that changed my life the most.

Authors including the Dalai Lama, Jeddu Krishnamurti, Swami Muktananda, Mahatma Gandhi, Paramahansa Yogananda, Sri Aurobindo, Ramana Maharshi, Maharishi Mahesh Yogi, Meher Baba,

Swami Rama, Sri Chinmoy, Chogyam Trungpa Rinpoche, Thich Nhat Hanh and Osho are people whose writings have affected me most profoundly. These are the teachers who have brought me my greatest realizations and helped me evolve the most. These are the teachers who have helped me the most to open my heart and to aspire to being of service to others.

There are many other authors I feel indebted to. After reading a book by one of these authors, you will look back and realize that you are an entirely different person than when you started reading it. These authors will shift your worldview so dynamically. Books by Ken Wilber, Dr. Deepak Chopra, Alan Watts, Paul Carus, Robert Thurman, Eckhart Tolle, Dr. Bruce Lipton, Dr. Albert Einstein, Ray Kurzweil, Don Miguel Ruiz, Dr. Masaru Emoto, Dr. Joe Dispenza, Dr. D.D. Palmer, Dr. B.J. Palmer, Rudolph Steiner, Henry David Thoreau and John Muir have profoundly changed me and the way I view the world. You will be just as excited to read the minds of brilliant women. I have been fortunate enough to enjoy work by enlightened and strong women like Marianne Williamson, Dr. Maya Angelou, Mother Theresa, Dr. Candace Pert, Alice Walker and Willa Cather.

I've also read many books on the subject of sacramental plant psychedelics. What I found was more than I could ever have imagined. By reading these pioneers who champion freedom of the mind, I became engaged in monologues and discoveries about politics, psychology, nature, Eastern wisdom, human evolution, human potentiality, botany, quantum physics and more. Authors like Dr. Timothy Leary, Alan Ginsberg, Dr. Gordon Wasson, Baba Ram Dass, Ken Kesey, Stephen Gaskin, Paul Krassner, Dr. John Lily, Dr. Stanislov Grof, Jack Kerouac, Terence McKenna, Dr. Richard Evans Schultes, David Jay Brown, Adam Gottlieb and the incomparable Aldous Huxley are all waiting for you girls to discover within the amazing books of your future library. There is a surprise around every corner.

When it comes to reading, my advice is leave "pop culture" behind. The way I see it, reading is a way to learn about life and how to live it. Make your reading sacred.

Reading is a way to get centered. You can connect with a book. You can connect with a wave of vibration from its author. You can evaluate things that great people thought were important enough to write about and share with humanity. A light bulb goes off, a lightning bolt strikes, a passion begins, brand new understandings and ways of seeing the world ensue, and you are transported to a new level of evolution and, literally, to a new you. That is the magic of books; that is the magic of reading.

We are living in a society today that is losing touch with the magic of books. There is such a bombardment of entertainment in society today that it is nearly impossible to avoid. It will take discipline for you to make reading a habit. The knowledge you will take away with you from books can open you up to extraordinary possibilities, ones you never imagined.

A lifetime of books awaits you—those books that chose me and that I am proud to pass on to you. For now though, we will read *Where the Wild Things Are* before I tuck you in for bed and kiss you goodnight. Sweet dreams my angels.

Love always,
All ways,
Dad

Jana
Burlingame Calif.
March 2011

Part V
Happiness

Ananda and Naia, age 1
Santa Cruz, Calif.
August 2009

California, I'm Coming Home

Ananda, Jana and Naia
Ontario, Canada
March 2011

The two girls grew up at the edge of the ocean and knew it was paradise, and better than Eden which was only a garden.

—Eve Babitz

June 2011

Dear girls,

Growing up in a big concrete city like New York made it harder for me in my youth to feel drawn to nature for nature's sake. It took getting a little older and wiser to realize how magnificent the nature in some places can be and to understand what an important role nature plays regarding one's overall quality of life and emotional disposition. When I visited Northern California I realized that it is one of those places. That's when I first really noticed how beautiful the trees, the plants and the flowers are there. Along with its brilliant sunshine, the beaches, mountains, lakes and hot springs create a diversity and beauty that makes California the canvas nature uses most to boast some of its greatest artworks. California from the border of Mexico to the border of Oregon still possesses unspoiled beauty.

One of my favorite authors, the great naturalist John Muir had this to say in his 1912 book, *Yosemite*: "Looking eastward from the summit of Pacheco Pass one shining morning, a landscape was displayed that after all my wanderings still appears as the most beautiful I have ever beheld. At my feet lay the Great Central Valley of California, level and flowery, like a lake of pure sunshine, forty or fifty miles wide, five hundred miles long, one rich furred garden of Compositae. And from the eastern boundary of this vast golden flowerbed rose the mighty Sierra, miles in height, and so gloriously colored and so radiant, it seemed not clothed with light, but wholly composed of it, like the wall of some celestial city..."

I can only imagine the grace witnessed through John Muir's eyes while gazing on the grandest of all scenes, the Mighty Sierra, as a blanket of golden light. In his words, one can almost smell the freshness of the Earth and feel the cool winds of dusk bringing scents of wild mountain flowers, cedar and eucalyptus. In a moment like that, there is a heightened sense of things and the ability to feel a more direct connection to the great universal design.

I feel so very grateful to have lived in California for 10 years of my life. I did not really fall in love with California until the first time I visited the Bay Area in the mid-'90s with my best friend Anthony. He was getting ready to relocate, so we took a vacation out west to San Francisco and the Monterey Peninsula. No place on earth had ever struck me so profoundly.

I have been through most of coastal California and a good portion of its inland areas now. It would be a magnificent experience to hike the Pacific Crest Trail through the Sierra Nevada with all three of you girls when you are old enough. I will be sure to first read *Dancing with Marmots: The Story of a New Zealand Firefighter's 2650-Mile Journey Along the Pacific Crest Trail from Mexico to Canada* before our trip.

Starting in the south, I love San Diego and all the little coastal towns like Encinitas, Del Mar and Solana Beach. I think it's definitely worth it to be near the ocean. Life is good here. People live healthy lives. On the way north from there to Los Angeles, you will find some other lovely coastal towns, like Laguna Niguel and Huntington Beach.

Los Angeles is a conundrum. Although there is a prevalence of materialism there, the city also has great things to take advantage of. There are awesome lifestyle disciplines that originate in Los Angeles, and it is certainly a haven for artistic people. Many of my favorite vegan and raw restaurants are in LA. I've mentioned some of these in a previous letter but want to mention them again here: Real Food Daily, Planet Raw, Euphoria Loves Rawvolution and Golden Mean top the list.

LA Neighborhoods I enjoy the most are Venice, West LA, Brentwood and Santa Monica, which was the last place we all lived together. There are many artistic and Bohemian communities in the city. I love to shop at the Goodwill and other thrift stores there. It is amazing what you can find.

One of my favorite pictures of Jana was taken on the beach in Santa Monica, (see the title page of part II Love, Love, Love.) It's a close up picture of her face with one of the wisest and most comforting smiles I've ever seen on a child. It reminds me of a quote from Sri Chinmoy that says, "God wants from me a very special favor: He wants me to teach my mind how to smile all the time."

There is also a focus on many spiritual disciplines in "the city of angels," and you could probably take a different course or seminar in any one of them every night of the year. Smog and traffic do unfortunately cast a dark shadow over the city. I remember being terrified I'd be stuck there permanently one time when I couldn't see the mountains that separate Hollywood from the Valley due to smog. I don't know if it's a place I would choose to live again, but it sure is a fun place to visit.

As you head north from LA, the first place that deserves some attention is Santa Barbara. Santa Barbara is situated on an east-west section of coastline, the longest section on the West Coast of the United States. The amazing little city lies between the steep rising Santa Ynez Mountains and the Pacific Ocean. Santa Barbara's climate is like the Mediterranean, and the city is widely known as the American Riviera. It is famous for a reason, as the beaches and weather are fantastic, and it is far enough away from LA to have its own vibe.

Just over the mountains from Santa Barbara is Ojai. Since Ojai is lined up with an east-west mountain range, it is one of the few towns in the world to have a "pink moment" occur as the sun is setting. The fading sunlight creates a brilliant shade of pink for several minutes on the Topa Topa Bluffs at the east end of the Ojai Valley, more than 6,000 feet high. What an enchanting way to spend a few minutes saying goodbye to each day. The city has declared itself "The Shangri-La of Southern California," referring to the similarities between its focus on health and spirituality and the fact that it was portrayed as the mystical sanctuary featured in the classic film based on James Hilton's novel *Lost Horizon*.

One of my favorite enlightened gurus and authors, Jeddu Krishnamurti, started his foundation in Ojai. He just happens to share his birthday of May 12 with Jana. Some have said that Krishnamurti indirectly established the intellectual and social focus of the Ojai Valley. From his arrival, he attracted people from all over the world who traveled here to interview him and attend his yearly talks in the Oak Grove in Meiners Oaks. Among those were Aldous Huxley, Dr. David Bohm, Jackson Pollack, Christopher Isherwood and Ann Morrow Lindbergh. Hollywood stars such as Charlie Chaplin, Greta Garbo and Charles Laughton also came to the valley to hear him, as his reputation grew worldwide.

Farther north and just off the coast, halfway between Los Angeles and San Francisco, is the picturesque little college town of San Luis Obispo. I enjoyed the energy I picked up on while visiting there. Heading north from SLO and slightly inland, you will pass through Paso Robles, which is becoming quite famous for producing great wines.

Heading north up the coast from San Luis Obispo brings you to San Simeon, the home of the Hearst Castle. The famous classic movie *Citizen Cane* is based on the life of William Randolph Hearst who built the Hearst Castle that was later nicknamed Xanadu from the poem by Coleridge. Hearst Castle would likely sell for several billion dollars today and drew comparison to the summer palace of Kubla Kahn, the ruler and Emperor of China in the 13th century, as mentioned in Coleridge's poem: "In Xanadu, did Kubla Khan a stately pleasure-dome decree." Hearst was a huge media mogul and built the castle after being inspired as a boy during a long trip to Europe.

About 60 miles up the coast from San Simeon is Big Sur. Big Sur is a place of poetic beauty: an Eden. Henry Miller wrote in *Big Sur and the Oranges of Hieronymus Bosch*, "Big Sur is the California that men dreamed of years ago, this is the Pacific that Balboa looked at from the Peak of Darien, and this is the face of the earth as the Creator intended it to look." Big Sur is to me a paradise on Earth, and paradise has been a hard place to find.

Big Sur is also home to the Esalen Institute. Walking down the foot-lit path to the meditation house at dusk, it looks like you are entering the magical Forest of the Elves. Words can barely describe the feeling of being there in person. Jana was at Esalen with your mom and I when she was only weeks old. This year Esalen is celebrating 50 years of being the center of the movement for human potential. I look forward to the day when I will get to spend time there together with all three of you girls.

Big Sur is a place where the mountains crash dramatically into the Pacific. The Monarch butterflies migrate to Big Sur every October and roost in the eucalyptus trees along the Big Sur River. The unique Henry Miller Memorial Library is on the East Side of Highway One just north of Esalen. On the west side of Highway One, just up the road is Nepenthe cafe and restaurant. What a great place to spend a day with views that challenge the imagination.

The state parks here should not be missed. Some of my favorites are Andrew Molera State Park, Julia Pfeiffer Burns State Park and Pfeiffer State Beach. I once drove from the center of Big Sur over the mountains to Highway 101. As I climbed the switchbacks through the redwoods, I could see the ocean behind me, and it was all so beautiful I thought I might be ascending into heaven. There is not enough that I can say about this mystical and magical place.

North of Big Sur is the quaint and exclusive town of Carmel where Clint Eastwood was mayor from 1986 to 1988. Carmel is beautiful, a neighbor to Pebble Beach and the famous Seventeen Mile Drive. Just north of Pebble Beach is Monterey where the great Monterey Jazz Festival happens every fall. John Steinbeck's famous classic novel *Cannery Row* is set in Monterey.

A bit farther up the coast is Santa Cruz where we all lived together for a wonderful year. Your mom and I had no car in Santa Cruz, so we took you three girls everywhere on our bicycles, riding behind us in our Schwinn bike attachments. Every Wednesday afternoon, we would bike to the downtown farmers' market and marvel over the stone fruit from Frog Hollow Farms and Kashiwase Farms. In the summer, there was an explosion of peaches, plums, pluots, nectarines and cherries, and that was just the beginning. I had the best English peas, sugar snap peas, heirloom tomatoes and varietals of what seemed to be every type of summer fruit and vegetable. It is an amazing market, especially in the summer.

I really loved living in Santa Cruz. It is alive with a cast of characters who are intent on expressing themselves in whatever fashion they please. It's for hippies, Bohemians, minimalists, surfers and it is university-driven. Logos, my favorite bookstore in the entire world, is in Santa Cruz. I have spent many hours on the lower level of Logos buying books on philosophy, Buddhism, Hinduism, Taoism, health, psychology and other more uniquely named categories. Educated and socially conscious people recycle multitudes of hard-to-find books in these categories and circulate them through the shelves of Logos.

Santa Cruz, Berkeley (A top choice of mine for where I hope you go to university some day) and the city of San Francisco itself are some very cool places with people who are more artistic, more socially conscious, more able to think independently, more Bohemian and more educated than people in all other places that I have lived. Two of my very favorite authors live in Soquel, a small town neighboring Santa Cruz. People drawn to this area felt to me like brothers and sisters in a way of thinking and a way of living. This area of California is a place where there is a collection of people who champion peace, justice, freedom, self-expression, art and love.

Another town to mention in this area is Half Moon Bay. It's a sleepy little beach town fairly close to San Francisco that plays annual host to the surf contest called Mavericks. Half Moon Bay is west of Silicon Valley, just over the mountain range and up the coast from Santa Cruz. It was so much fun taking you to the Pumpkin Festival held there each fall season. There are always fairs and festivals happening throughout California, but this is one of my favorites. In addition to the brightly colored pumpkins, there are hundreds of artists in the street displaying their great work.

We would get there early in the morning and walk through the ocean mist and fog while warming up by sipping hot apple cider. That fog would turn into sunshine by late morning, and we had a great time before the masses rolled in. We took the mountain pass home to San Mateo in the early afternoon, your mother and I laughing at the traffic that had amassed and was inching slowly forward in the opposite direction. Another Bay Area fair every Labor Day weekend is the King Mountain Arts Fair where artists set up their work on a trail through the redwoods. I felt so privileged to be there with you young girls.

We lived in San Mateo when Jana was born and in the neighboring town Burlingame when Naia and Ananda were born. San Mateo and Burlingame are quite lovely places to live and are situated about 15 miles south of San Francisco. We had the greatest apartment with a '70s design to it. You girls all spent time as babies in the sunshine, splashing around in blow-up pools on our balcony. I opened my first solo chiropractic practice in San Mateo. We kept Jana in a crib, playing in the reception area. We were the quintessential family of three at the time.

The city of San Francisco is fantastic. As the mountain range that protects the peninsula comes to an end just south of the city, the fog can freely roll in off the ocean. Because of the topography of the city, there are microclimates and weather patterns that make specific neighborhoods either foggy or sunny the majority of the time. The fog starts rolling in off the coast just south of the city. It flows through Pacifica and San Francisco across the Golden Gate into most of the coastal North Bay and up the coast to the northern counties. The fog adds a mystical quality.

San Francisco has always had great appeal for me. It is small and picturesque, bordering the Pacific Ocean with many distinct and diverse neighborhoods, such as Golden Gate Park, The Marina, Nob Hill, The Presidio, Pacific Heights, Haight-Ashbury, Chinatown, Japantown, SoMa, The Tenderloin, North Beach, Ghirardelli Square, The Mission, Noe Valley, Balboa Park, Cow Hollow, The Fillmore, Fisherman's Wharf, The Sunset, Little Russia, Twin Peaks and The Castro. The Castro was and still is a center for Gay Rights as immortalized by Sean Penn playing Harvey Milk in the great movie *Milk*. There is always something awesome to do in San Francisco.

Concerts and first-rate artistic performances in Stern Grove play for free every Sunday in the summer.

Jana saw her first ballet in San Francisco. It was the *Nutcracker* at the San Francisco Ballet. She loved every minute of it. Another of my favorite bookstores is in San Francisco and is named Green Apple books. It's another one of those revolving door bookstores with books to enlighten the soul. There is something quite amazing about San Francisco. I love the people, the vibe, the energy, the diversity, the aesthetics, the sunshine, the fog, the food, the Golden Gate Bridge, the Transamerica Building and the cold summer. As Mark Twain once said, "The coldest winter I ever spent was my summer in San Francisco." I might add that he also was quoted in a letter once, saying, "I am sorry this letter is so long, I didn't have time to make it shorter."

John Phillips of the '60s vocal group The Mommas and the Poppas wrote the famous song, "San Francisco" reminding us to wear flowers in our hair. I think the city still represents the peace and love vibe of the late 1960s. Back then "Love ins," "Be ins" and concerts in Golden Gate Park were part of the movement for peace. There were Beat poets, musicians and artists, some of whom are still there, as well as the children raised by them who are now adults. The food is great, too. San Francisco is a mecca for vegetarians, vegans and raw foodies, and has some amazing restaurants, many of which I enjoyed with you girls when we lived there.

East of San Francisco is Berkeley. This is my favorite spot in the East Bay. It is another center for social consciousness. The university there has been a driving force for non-traditional education and free thinkers. We spent a lovely, sunshine-filled morning at the Berkeley University Botanical Garden plant sale. A truly remarkable place, the gardens now have more than 10,000 species of plants that collectively originate from all seven continents. It was officially established in 1890. We found such beautiful plants to take home and had a lovely family day planned around something simple and natural.

We discovered the observatory on the university campus and were astounded at the view of the entire bay and city. If I could do it all over again, Berkeley would in all likelihood be the school of my choice.

Berkeley is full of Bohemians. There, a priority is placed on self-expression and living life. The university is the most consistently well-ranked university in the world overall. It has the highest number of distinguished graduate programs ranked in the top 10 in their fields. It also has a reputation for student activism that stemmed from the free speech movement of the 1960s. Another famous Bay Area used bookstore that was established and flourished in this era is in Berkeley. Founded by a man named Moe Moskowitz in 1959, it is appropriately named Moe's Books. It has become a landmark and beloved institution in Berkeley, appearing in the movie *The Graduate*, and it is just a stone's throw from the campus.

To the north of San Francisco are some magical places. The Golden Gate Bridge itself is an incredible sight. As you cross it, the expansive Pacific Ocean tempts one's imagination to think of what may lie beyond it. It is quite something to cross it with the dramatic landscapes, scenery and views that surround you. Sausalito and Mill Valley are lovely towns, and are conveniently close to the city. Cavallo Point, where I worked for a short time, is a resort that sits near the Golden Gate Bridge in Sausalito with perfect views looking back on the twinkling lights of San Francisco.

Some of my other favorite spots in the North Bay are Stinson Beach, Mount Tamalpais, Muir Beach, Muir Woods and the Zen Center at Green Gulch. Muir Woods, which is named in tribute for the previously mentioned naturalist John Muir, is a national landmark and is treasured for giant redwoods taller than 250 feet! The oldest of these trees are estimated to be 1,200 years old, and to put that in perspective, means they may have been alive during the ancient Chinese Tang Dynasty.

Marin County is beautiful, affluent and has a very natural energy to it. North and northeast of Marin is Sonoma County. On the coast is Bodega Bay where the famous Alfred Hitchcock movie *The Birds* was filmed. Sonoma is also one of the more famous valleys for wine, although nearby Napa takes all the glory. I love wine from these and other nearby regions with Cabernet and full-bodied Syrah inland and Pinot Noir from the Sonoma Coast and Anderson Valley, where every year in May, you can enjoy the Pinot Noir Festival. St. Helena is a town near Napa that I enjoy, and also close to Napa is the Harbin Hot Springs Retreat.

Harbin has natural hot springs and they are very hot! It takes me about 5 to 10 minutes to inch my naked body into the hot pool for the first time. There is also a cold pool with water coming right off the close by mountain stream. It is great therapy for your muscles and connective tissues to alternate back and forth in the hot and cold pools, as it creates a vascular flush and causes blood to flow more readily into any injured areas. Whenever I visit, I do this for several hours. Afterward, everything in my body feels relaxed and clear of tension. Nudity is optional at Harbin and also at the Esalen Institute's baths and pools. The best part is that nobody cares. It's a great feeling to be able to swim and bathe naked. What could be more natural than that?

During the time your mother was pregnant with Naia and Ananda, we discovered Mendocino County. In the little town of Fort Bragg, your mother spent time at The Living Light Institute becoming qualified as a raw vegan chef and chef instructor. I was proud of how dedicated and passionate she was about her pursuits there. Every weekend for two months, I would drive several hours north from San Francisco through Anderson Valley and then up the coast to Mendocino, listening to Ken Wilber's 10 CD set, *Kosmic Consciousness*.

Ken Wilber is the most widely translated academic writer in America, with 25 books translated in some 30 foreign languages. He is the first philosopher-psychologist to have his collected works published while still alive and also he is the co-founder of The Center for World Spirituality. When you discover Ken Wilber's work you will understand that my drives up to Mendocino listening to him were life-changing and amazingly mind-altering.

Mendocino County and Humboldt County are famous for the cultivation of marijuana. Two-thirds of the economy in those parts is based on growing it. The state parks of Mendocino County are also of note and are great places to spend time when you need to get away and connect with nature. These northern coastal California counties are as alive with nature and wildlife as any place I have ever seen. I have yet to drive the entire coast of California, but destiny will call again, hopefully with you girls along for the ride.

The northernmost county on the coast is Del Norte County. The redwoods there are known to be as tall as 350 feet and were used as a set in part of the Star Wars film *Return of the Jedi*. East of Mendocino and Humboldt is the northern part of the great central valley that John Muir so vividly describes in his book, *Yosemite*. Recently, some of the oldest and tallest trees have been found in Sequoia National Park in the Sierra Nevada Mountains and have been recorded at an astonishing 3,200 years old.

I am in love with California, and I know you will be as well. Never forget, no matter where in the world you might be, that the three of you are California girls in your heart and soul. You were born in California, and you deserve the sunshine, the people, the freedom of thought and the energy that this special place in the world has to offer. In his "Promise to California," Walt Whitman wrote, "Soon I travel toward you, to remain, to teach robust American love; for I know very well that I and robust love belong among you, inland and along the Western sea…" I must say that good old Walt and I share the same sentiment. Although I am not there in body at this moment of writing, I am always there in spirit. Alive or not, my return there is inevitable.

Love always,
Dad

Jana
Santa Cruz, Calif.
May 2009

'Twas the Night of Loving Kindness

Ananda, Naia and Jana
Brooklyn, N.Y.
December 2011

December 22, 2010

Dear girls,
Here is a holiday poem I wrote to you that I thought would embody a more sincere spirit of the holidays.

'Twas the night of loving kindness, and all through the land,
Everyone was accepting of their fellow man,
Compassion was in the hearts of all with great care,
In hopes that world peace soon would be there.

The children were dreaming with all of their might,
That world hunger would end by the coming daylight
And mamma in the garden, and I in my grace,
Were praying and meditating to help make the world a better place.

All the wars and exploitation, and the death of good men,
Will certainly and instantly come to an end
Where is our wise savior to lead us to glory?
Destroy all our fears and end all our worry?

He lives inside you in the thoughts of your mind,
Through your actions, and your love and decisions to be kind
Just a smile can change a life in an instant, you'll see,
And helping out people will fill you with glee.

So remember your heart is filled with God's light,
Be loving kindness to all, and to all a good night.

—Adam Kleinberg

Music Makes the World Go Round

Ananda and Naia
Ontario, Canada
March 2011

Music gives a soul to the universe, wings to the mind,
flight to the imagination and life to everything.

—Plato

December 2011

Dear girls,

This past spring, Jana and I went to see my Aunt Marilyn sing at the Lenox Lounge in Harlem. Marilyn has chosen a musical life and she is quite a wonderful jazz singer. Over the last 30 years, I have been able to watch her perform in various New York City venues, and she has introduced me to many great musicians she has played with, including Harry Whitaker, Hiram Bullock, Daryl Jones, Alex Blake and Herbie Hancock.

Naia and Ananda were too young to join us, so your grandmother Judy agreed to babysit while Jana and I went to watch the early set. I had to park about four long blocks away from the venue, and we were in a rush to get there on time. Jana was wearing quite a fancy white dress and white shoes. I carried her on my shoulders, her long, golden blonde hair bouncing up and down as we walked quickly across 125th street in Harlem. I don't remember seeing another white person on our entire walk in either direction. As mentioned, I grew up in the Bronx, so I tend to walk fearlessly in any neighborhood, but we did catch our share of territorial stares. I imagine Jana may have looked like a little Nordic princess visiting an African nation.

Once inside the lounge, we sat up front, so we could see the jazz musicians make love to their instruments and Marilyn opened her set with one of my favorite songs, "Our Love Is Here to Stay." I immediately started crying but didn't let Jana see me because I wanted her to enjoy the music.

My tears of joy came from a combination of things. On my 13th birthday, my Aunt Marilyn serenaded me at my bar mitzvah party. I felt so proud that she was still performing and doing what she really loves to do. Also, I was overwhelmed at the full circle of life, listening to her sing to my daughter and me in front of a packed house. The title of the song struck me about my relationship with all three of you girls and that it is indeed very clear: "Our Love Is Here to Stay." All of a sudden, a wave of deep emotion swept over me, but underneath all the emotion, the music itself was opening my heart and soul.

What would we all do without music in the world? Life would be missing something so fundamental in its absence. Within my heart, I have the burning desire to provide for you girls a life filled with music, and I hope I can introduce you to all that I love about it. Columnist Ian Mathers writes in *Stylus Magazine*, "There are magic moments that arise when listening to a piece of music that strikes that special chord inside. That pounding drum intro; a clanging guitar built-up to an anthemic chorus; that strange glitchy noise you've never quite been able to figure out; that first kiss or heartbreak; a well-turned rhyme that reminds you of something in your own past so much, it seems like it was written for you—all of those little things that make people love music. Every music lover has a collection of these seconds in his or her head."

Music really does make the world-go-round!

I asked this question to a few of the great musicians Marilyn introduced me to: "If you were choosing a first instrument, what would it be?" They have all given the same answer, which is, "the piano" without hesitation. I would like all three of you to play the piano. I want you to play any instruments you like, but the piano first. Sometimes I find myself fantasizing that in the future I am watching and listening to you girls playing my favorite piano piece. It's hard for me to hold back the tears. My favorite contemporary musicians all play the piano. Billy Joel, Elton John, Paul McCartney, John Legend, Alicia Keys and Stevie Wonder have all aroused deep emotions in me with their music.

Creating and performing original music could be the finest artistic accomplishment that humans are capable of. People dedicate their lives to it. Music requires poetry, rhythm, rhyme, accuracy, imagination, composition, humor, sentimentality, soulfulness, dedication, practice, patience, understanding, insight, intuition, passion, confidence and talent. You girls already love to sing. We sing together all the time.

I want you to appreciate all types of music. Don't judge any music, but choose carefully what you listen to. There is a specific vibrational frequency that comes through music. I try to listen to music that inspires me, that lifts my spirits or evokes emotion and that has a beneficent force behind it. There has been extensive research presented in the mind-blowing book *The Secret Life of Plants* by Peter Tompkins and Christopher Bird, showing how plants thrived or not when exposed to certain kinds of music. When played compositions by Bach, the plants thrived, but the plants' growth was curtailed by hard rock and roll.

Once again, the book *The Hidden Messages in Water* by Dr. Masaru Emoto shows stunning correlations between the types of music played, and the quality and beauty of the ice crystals that formed upon water freezing. Samples of distilled water that had been exposed to Beethoven's Fifth Symphony versus "heavy metal" music had ice crystal formations that were clearly beautiful versus ugly.

Listen to, read and understand the lyrics of an artist's song if you want to see into that person's heart. When focusing on reading the lyrics of a song alone without the amusement of the music one can appreciate the lyrics for the poetry that they are. Stevie Wonder wrote, "Another Star," "Sunshine in Their Eyes" and "I am Singing." Billy Joel wrote, "She's Got a Way," "Scenes from an Italian Restaurant" and "New York State of Mind." Elton John wrote, "I Guess That's Why They Call It the Blues" and "Goodbye Yellow Brick Road." The Beatles wrote, "All You Need Is Love" and John Lennon wrote, "Instant Karma," and my favorite of his "Watching the Wheels."

When the poetry of music is then paired with the composition of the music itself, a magic alchemy occurs; there is a transmutation of words, notes, phrases and melodies into art so sweet and beautiful, it pervades the soul. When I think of the ways music will help you cope and move on in your life, I can cope and move on in my own. When I think of the ways that music will touch your hearts, then my heart is touched. When I think of the ways music will light up your days, my days light up like the brightness of the sun.

Music has deep and moving effects on politics, and on the shaping of culture and society. Stevie Wonder wrote "Black Man" to commemorate the role that all races have played in shaping the United States and to remind us that this world was made for all men, women and children. His words echo inside me whenever I witness racial discrimination or come across bigoted people.

Neil Young wrote the song "Ohio" just weeks after the non-violent protests at Kent State by students against the United States' occupation of Cambodia. The protests resulted in four students shot to death and nine others wounded by the Ohio National Guard. Hundreds of universities, colleges and high schools closed throughout the United States due to a strike of 4 million students, and the event helped sway the public opinion at an already socially combative time over the role of the United States in the Vietnam War. Crosby, Stills, Nash and Young wrote, "Find the Cost of Freedom." This song was originally slated for the last scene of the movie "Easy Rider" with Peter Fonda, Dennis Hopper and Jack Nicholson but instead was released on the B-side of "Ohio," as its lyrics were also fittingly about Kent State and in protest to the war.

Woodstock could be the greatest musical gathering of all time. It was billed as three days of peace, love and music. Richie Havens, Santana, Crosby, Stills and Nash, The Who, Jefferson Airplane, Janice Joplin, Jimi Hendrix, The Grateful Dead, Joe Cocker, The Band, Joan Baez and Ravi Shankar are just some of the great musicians that graced the stage at this crux of the free love movement. It showed the world just how powerful music is and how far reaching the message of music can be. It was an event that will continue to be memorialized for generations to come.

On a blog at *Rock's Backpages*, Barney Hoskins wrote, "The question now is: is Woodstock *still* too big for the world to comprehend and contextualize? It remains the defining assembly of rock's half-century lifespan, an unprecedented gathering of at least 300,000 young, longhaired, raggedly-clad Americans 'going up the country' in New York's Catskill's mountains, searching for answers, hoping for transcendence... and finding *what*, exactly?"

Your grandmother and grandfather were on their way to Woodstock, but they never made it because the New York Thruway was turned into a 100-mile-long parking lot due to the volume of people trying to make their way to the event in the summer heat of

August 1969. I was 13 months old. In the midst of another meaningless war that was killing our young boys and countless Vietnamese men, women and children, there were three days of peace, love and music, and as a result perhaps the most principled political and philosophical statement that music has ever made.

On the other end of the spectrum, about 15 years later, rap music and the hip hop movement evolved in front of my eyes as an '80s teenager on the streets of the northeast Bronx. I really enjoyed it, and it was new and fun during its first years with artists like The Sugar Hill Gang, Curtis Blow, Grandmaster Flash, The Beastie Boys, Run DMC and later Public Enemy and De La Soul. It gave urban minority youth a voice that did not exist previously. Public Enemy's "Fight the Power" sent an important political message and débuted in Spike Lee's poignant movie, *Do the Right Thing*. But most rap music has deteriorated from its clever roots due to glorification of violence, drug use, the gangster mentality, sexism, racism, infatuation with materialism and excessive profanity.

It wasn't until later in my life that I discovered the depth and beauty of classical music. It is a form of music that I will do all I can to help you fall in love with. We recently saw an octet from the Toronto Symphony Orchestra while staying in Kingston, Ontario, and you girls stared in awe from the front pew of the church that hosted the show. You witnessed first-class musicians in loving relationship with their instruments. Some of my favorite composers are Debussy, Bach, Mozart, Beethoven, Vivaldi, Schubert, Rachmaninoff, Brahms, Tchaikovsky, Handel, Dvorak, Liszt, Verde, Strauss, Stravinsky, Ravel, Puccini and Gershwin. I believe there is no music that compares with the quality and rapture of classical music. The absolute depth of emotion comes through the music straight from the soul of the composer.

Classical music reaches the highest peaks and the lowest depths of the range of human feelings and experience. It really takes a talented and insightful poet to try to describe how one is affected by music that is so beautiful and that typically has no lyrics. If you girls would like to play for me someday, two of my favorite pieces are by Debussy: "Claire de Lune" for piano, and "Arabesque" for flute and harp. The first time I heard Arabesque I imagined that if a musical piece could embody the lives of you girls, I would want it to be this magical, gentle and profound one.

Jazz appeals to me in many different ways. It is a true improvisational art form. It bends the norm into something a little different. It challenges conventionality. It doesn't play by the rules. Jazz has a rich history with its roots in the southern USA and eventually spawned fuel for the Beat poets of New York City. Writers like Jack Kerouac and Allen Ginsberg felt that jazz was a way of life, a completely different way to approach the creative process.

In his only successful book, Go, Beat author John Clellon Holmes wrote, "In this modern jazz, they heard something rebel and nameless that spoke for them, and their lives knew a gospel for the first time. It was more than music, it became an attitude toward life, and a way of walking, a language and a costume; and these introverted kids... now felt somewhere at last."

The types of music that I enjoy include works from a long list of artists that have touched me, but the artist that has affected me most profoundly is the master himself, Stevie Wonder.

Stevie is a virtuoso, a poet, a spiritual force of love and hope, a composer and a talent unlike any other. Ask anyone who really knows his music and they will agree. India Arie sings it best in her song "Wonder-ful," delivering the type of praise upon him that I have felt he deserves my whole life. The first time I heard it, I had tears running down my face. All types of artists from hip-hop to alternative rock have remade his songs, including George Michael, Coolio and the Red Hot Chili Peppers.

The great jazz pianist Chick Corea said of Stevie, upon his induction into the Apollo legends hall of fame, "I consider him to be one of the most important musicians who ever hit planet Earth. His music contains a human rights message because it goes above any kind of religion or philosophy. It's a thing all of humanity can get behind. I consider him a guiding light." If I could spend one day with any human being on the planet, your daddy would spend a day with Stevie Wonder!

Some of my other very favorite artists include Sting/The Police, Billy Joel, Elton John, the Beatles (and solo works of John Lennon, Paul McCartney and George Harrison), Richie Havens, Marvin Gaye, Ella Fitzgerald, India Arie, Lenny Kravitz, The Red Hot Chili Peppers, The Foo Fighters, Anita Baker, Van Morrison, James Taylor, Steely Dan, U2, Michael McDonald and The Doobie Brothers, Jack Johnson, John Mayer, Ray Charles, Bill Withers, Earth Wind and Fire, Crosby, Stills and Nash, Joni Mitchell, George Benson, Santana, Squeeze, Simon and Garfunkel, Pearl Jam, The B-52's, REM, George Michael, Tony Bennett, Michael Jackson, Nat King Cole, Mel Tourme, Sammy Davis Jr., Frank Sinatra, Stevie Ray Vaughn, Andrea Bocelli and, of course, your Great Auntie Marilyn.

After many years of studying Indian spiritual traditions, within the last decade I have discovered Indian classical and devotional music. When we are in the car, you girls often ask me to play "Om Namah Shivaya" by Govindas from the album *Endless Surrender*. It brings me so much joy to hear you sing this song. I can only hope my passion and love for music trickles down to you girls and that you fall in love with creating music as much as listening to it.

Of course, it is inevitable that you will listen to horrible popular music that your generation creates, just like I did and my parents did, and the generations that came before them did. But music really has changed a lot in the last 20 years. Very few artists actually write anymore. Television shows like *American Idol* use teams of people to package artists who then come to the stage like a well-marketed microwave dinner. I'm afraid the artistry of creating and performing something original is quickly dying.

Find the music that touches your heart. Find the lyrics that teach you lessons about life, love, God and spirit. Listen to the music that helps you identify with the human condition and that means something more than the superficial. Music will make your heart sing. It is innately within your spirit. It is one with your soul. Hopefully we will all soon be blessed again to listen to your Great Auntie Marilyn singing her favorite tunes. After hearing her sing periodically for my entire life, I know as usual that she will knock our socks off!

Love always,
Dad

Jana's First Poem — A Haiku

Hello Jell-O
On the window
Goodbye Jell-O, Smello.
Love Jana

Jana
Wave Hill, Riverdale, Bronx, N.Y.
June 2011

Do You Smell Popcorn?

Ananda
Ontario, Canada
December 2011

Film as dream, film as music, no art passes our conscience in the way film does, and goes directly to our feelings, deep down into the dark rooms of our souls.

—Ingmar Bergman

Dear girls,

I have always loved the movies. As kids, my friends and I would sometimes pay for one movie and then sneak into one, two and, on some occasions, even three more movies before we left the theater that day.

A film is a piece of art. When you examine a film and all that goes into it, you realize how visionary those who make them must be. The music, the cinematography, the costumes and a host of other factors must come together to create something with synergy, something that just works. Viewing a film is, in an artistic sense, like looking through the eyes of God. You get to see creation. It is the creation of someone's vision.

The movies listed in this letter are movies that moved me, inspired me and played a part in influencing my life. Some will make you cry, and others are sure to make you laugh. It seems like the very best movies make you do both and somehow can change your life by instantly changing the way you see the world.

I recently saw quite an emotionally moving documentary called *George Harrison: Living in the Material World*. The great director Martin Scorsese masterfully paints an honest and intimate portrait of George as one the great musicians, poets and sages of our time. After so much fame with the Beatles, George led a very spiritual life. I learned so much from this film's inside perspectives about the way this famous man chose to live and what he prioritized.

The following movies are not documentaries, though. No, these are the popcorn movies that Hollywood creates with the magic that only its wizards can conjure up. It has taken me more than 35 years to create this list of my all-time favorite movies. I want to pass it onto you girls. The really good movies, the magic ones, are few and far between. I hope this list saves you a lot of time in your search for inspiring entertainment.

Mr. Smith Goes to Washington. This is the magic of Frank Capra and Jimmy Stewart, giving us a glimpse behind the political machine.

Jimmy Stewart gives one of the most sincere performances ever captured in a film.

Good Will Hunting. This is one of my very favorites with amazing dialogue and performances highlighted by the brilliant Robin Williams, along with the boys from Boston, Matt Damon and Ben Affleck.

Slumdog Millionaire. It is impossible not to feel grateful for your life after experiencing this incredibly written film. In my opinion, it was the best film of the decade.

Dead Poet's Society. Once again, the brilliant Robin Williams inspires in this coming-of-age Ivy League prep school story. *Yawp*!

Braveheart. Mel Gibson's epic with incredible cinematography captures the liberation of Scotland from England. "What will you do without freedom?!"

Into the Wild. John Krakauer's book, from which the film was made, tells the true story of a very unique young man full of love for life and expressing his love for adventure, nature and solitude. This film contains a brilliant performance by Emile Hirsch, equally brilliant direction from Sean Penn, and is musically accented by acoustic songs from Eddie Vedder of the band Pearl Jam.

Billy Jack. A sentimental favorite film of mine, Tom Laughlin's heartbreaking tale of an ex-Green Beret who searches for his spiritual side in the late 1960s while fighting small-town segregation and racism. Billy says, "Do you know what mental toughness is? Well, mental toughness is the ability to accept the fact that you're human and that you're going to make mistakes—lots of 'em—all your life. And some of them are gonna hurt people that you love very badly. But you have the guts to accept the fact that you ain't perfect. And you don't let your mistakes crush you and keep you from doing the very best that you can."

It's a Wonderful Life. A Christmas miracle with the most heartfelt performances by Jimmy Stewart and Donna Reed. This is another brilliantly directed classic from Frank Capra.

The Hurricane. Based on the true story of the boxer Rubin Hurricane Carter and the racism that incarcerated him for a crime he didn't commit with the phenomenal Denzel Washington at his very best.

American Beauty. Incredible acting by the entire cast highlighted by Chris Cooper, Annette Benning and the Oscar-winning performance of Kevin Spacey. It also has an amazing script, fantastic score and the brilliant direction of Sam Mendes.

Life is Beautiful. Roberto Benigni shows off his absolute genius, making you laugh and cry in this amazing story of love and family.

Sideways. An Oscar-snubbed, sincere and vulnerable performance by one of my favorite actors, Paul Giamatti. This is a wonderfully written script with great laughs and great supporting performances by Thomas Hayden Church, Virginia Madsen and Sandra Oh. Beautiful cinematography highlights the wine regions of California.

Forrest Gump. This film is an instant classic with Oscar-wining Tom Hanks leading the way through a history of the modern U. S. from the 1950s to its present day with a time-matching soundtrack and one of the most original stories ever written for the big screen. "Momma always said life is like a box of chocolates, you never know what you're gonna get."

Snatch. This is a brilliant, character-acted, Guy Ritchie-created London underworld caper. Brad Pitt plays a great Irish gypsy who somehow gets the last laugh.

The Professional. Contains captivating and career-making performances by a young Natalie Portman and by Jean Reno as well as an amazing performance by the gifted and tumultuous Gary Oldman.

Silence of the Lambs. Academy award-winner Anthony Hopkins creates one of the most complex characters to ever hit the big screen in Hannibal Lecter. This is a brilliantly suspenseful script with other great performances by Jodi Foster and Ted Levine as Buffalo Bill.

Say Anything. This film is a magical connection of a young John

Cusack with the writing brilliance of Cameron Crowe. This is a coming-of-age high school tale with the exquisite Ione Skye as the object of Lloyd Dobbler's affections. This sweet little film has some of the greatest dialogue. "She's gone. She gave me a pen. I gave her my heart, she gave me a pen."

Ferris Bueller's Day Off. This is the quintessential John Hughes high school fantasy film, starring a young and irresistible Mathew Broderick. "The question isn't "what are we going to do;" the question is "what aren't we going to do?"

The Matrix. A brilliantly written script drives this larger-than-life thriller that allows us to look behind the dream into a dystopian reality of a digital world and the battle of man versus machine. This is one of the greatest, mind-blowing films of all time.

A Clockwork Orange. Stanley Kubrick's classic was banned in England for nearly 30 years due to its violence. This is one of the best films of the century with twists of harsh irony and a saucy young Malcolm McDowell who ignited his career in the starring role.

The Shawshank Redemption. Morgan Freeman's narration brings Steven King's novella to life with Tim Robbins giving a career-best performance in a brilliantly written, acted and directed film.

The Black Stallion. There is very little dialogue in this sleepy, sweet film about a boy and a stallion shipwrecked alone together on a tropical island. The cinematography is in my opinion among the best ever.

Night on Earth. In this unknown gem, Jim Jarmusch delivers comic genius with an all-star international cast, highlighting five taxi rides from Los Angeles, New York, Paris, Rome and Helsinki.

Johnny Stecchino. Stecchino is Italian for "toothpick." Here is another brilliantly written and acted, laugh-out-loud comedy by the amazing Roberto Benigni.

Shine. This is the true story of the virtuoso pianist David Helfgott, portrayed by the one-and-only, Oscar-winning Geoffrey Rush.

Million Dollar Baby. Clint Eastwood won the Oscar directing a heartbreaking masterpiece by Paul Haggis with Oscar-winning acting performances by Hillary Swank and the incomparable Morgan Freeman.

Chocolat. This sweet little story of life in a little French village shows the rigid religious morals that are so often misused to segregate rather than integrate, with great performances by Juliette Binoche, Alfred Molina, Johnny Depp and Judi Dench.

Fantasia. Watching this film is one of my earliest memories. It is Disney's animated all time fantasy classic set to classical musical that made its début in 1940.

The Manchurian Candidate. Frank Sinatra, Angela Lansbury and Laurence Harvey give amazing performances in this dark and intelligent political thriller that was banned in many countries after its release in 1962.

Bruce Almighty. A classic comedic performance by the absolute one-and-only Jim Carrey and the versatile Morgan Freeman as God. I don't know that anyone has ever made me laugh as much or as hard in a movie as Jim Carrey.

Seabiscuit. A true story of the horseracing equivalent of David and Goliath with amazing acting by Jeff Bridges, Chris Cooper and Tobey Maguire.

An Officer and a Gentleman. A career-solidifying performance by an amazingly handsome and raw, young Richard Gere in this sweet but solemn film about army life and love. It also has a show-stealing and Oscar-winning performance by Lou Gossett Jr. as drill sergeant Foley.

Cinderella Man. A true story of the New Jersey fighter Jim Braddock who battles through injury and the Great Depression to get another chance at greatness and to provide a better life for his family. There is fantastic chemistry from director Ron Howard, along with the acting by Russell Crowe, Renee Zellweger and Paul Giamatti.

The Notebook. Ryan Gosling and Rachel McAdams ignite the

screen with their young love and passion for each other in the adaptation of the sweet novel by Nicholas Sparks. This is one of the greatest, most touching love stories on film.

Avatar. James Cameron shares his vision of other worlds where there is a core spirituality that runs through the tribal, alien society. This film is a visual feast.

Glengarry Glen Ross. An all-star cast takes David Mamet's screenplay off the charts. Al Pacino, Kevin Spacey, Jack Lemmon, Ed Harris, Alan Arkin, Jonathan Pryce and Alec Baldwin are at their sharpest in this great little character-driven film.

The Hustler. Paul Newman plays fast Eddie Felson in this 1961 classic about an up-and-coming pool player trying to dethrone Jackie Gleason who plays the legendary Minnesota Fats.

Road to Perdition. Tom Hanks, Paul Newman, Jude Law and Daniel Craig are all masterful in this story of revenge and a boy's relationship with his father. Once again, Sam Mendes masterfully directs.

The Pianist. Adrien Brody wins the Oscar in this film directed by Roman Polanski about the true story of the survival of pianist Wladyslaw Szpilman through the Holocaust.

Schindler's List. Steven Spielberg won his first Oscar for directing this true story of the Holocaust with powerful performances by Liam Neeson, Ralph Fines and Ben Kingsley.

Rocky. Sylvester Stallone's classic won the Oscar for best film in 1977, telling the story of a down-and-out boxer who gets a chance to find self-respect and through the process finds love in his life. Bill Conti delivers one of the most inspiring scores ever on film.

Jaws. This is one of the greatest suspense thrillers ever with young master director Steven Spielberg at the helm. Roy Scheider, Richard Dreyfuss and Robert Shaw all give masterful performances.

Milk. Sean Penn wins his well-deserved Oscar for playing Harvey Milk who was the first openly gay elected official. Milk shows us that the oppression of the gay community was as strong as racial oppression and highlights the fight that originated in San Francisco. Gus

Van Sant is as masterful directing this film as he was in *Good Will Hunting*.

The Champ. This heartbreaking remake featuring a young Rick Schroder, Faye Dunaway and Jon Voight shows the unconditional love that only a young child could have for a parent.

The Lord of the Rings (Trilogy). Peter Jackson shares his uncompromising vision of J.R. R. Tolkien's trilogy of fantasy novels. The final film won 11 Oscars, including Best Director and Best Film. Popcorn movies at their best!

La Dolce Vita. Fellini's homage to the sweet life in Rome in 1960.

Random Harvest. Ronald Coleman stars in this heart-aching story of a man who loses his memory but through an irony of fate keeps the self-sacrificing dedication of the woman who loves him.

Lost Horizon. Ronald Coleman stars in this tale of lost travelers who happen upon the timeless and enlightened paradise of Shangri-La high in the mountains of the Himalayas. Based on the novel by James Hilton.

Pulp Fiction. This film made Quentin Tarantino the household name that he is today with incredibly creative dialogue and tremendous irony. This film has great monologues by Samuel L. Jackson, reinvents the career of John Travolta, and includes a great and hysterical cameo by my very favorite actor to impersonate, Christopher Walken.

Big. Tom Hanks charmed the world in this film about a boy who gets transformed into a man and has to suddenly fend for himself and learn the lessons of life.

Swingers. John Favreau brought himself and his buddy Vince Vaughn instant fame with this hilarious LA movie about a guy trying to break into the scene.

A Bronx Tale. Robert Deniro directs and costars with Chazz Palminteri in his story of the Bronx in 1960 where a local mob boss befriends a young boy.

Scent of a Woman. This film finally gave Al Pacino the Oscar he had deserved for so long. This film is another great coming of age story with a great performance by Chris O'Donnell.

Jerry Maguire. This is Cameron Crowe's *pièce de résistance*, the story of a man who suddenly grows a conscience as a top athlete's agent. Tom Cruise, Rene Zellwegger and Cuba Gooding Jr. turn in inspiring performances.

Match Point. Woody Allen pays homage to Alfred Hitchcock with this amazingly well written and satisfying psychological thriller. Scarlett Johansson is at her sexiest.

The Breakfast Club. This movie is another of John Hughes's great high school stories with brilliant dialogue and character acting by a young, all-star cast led by Judd Nelson, Emilio Estevez, Molly Ringwald, Ally Sheedy and Anthony Michael Hall.

The Nutty Professor. Jerry Lewis is at his comic peak playing the contrasting roles of the nutty professor and his alter ego Buddy Love.

Risky Business. This is the movie that began the launch of the megastar status of Tom Cruise.

Catch Me if You Can. Leonardo Dicaprio, Tom Hanks, Martin Sheen and Christopher Walken are directed by Steven Spielberg in this amazing true story about Frank Abagnale Jr. who, before his 19th birthday, successfully conned millions of dollars worth of checks as a Pan Am pilot, doctor and legal prosecutor.

Stripes. Early Bill Murray is at his funniest in this comedy about army life. "That's the fact, Jack!"

One Flew Over the Cuckoo's Nest. In this adaptation of Ken Kesey's classic novel, Jack Nicholson wins his first of three Best Actor Oscars. The inspiration for this film came while Kesey was working on the night shift at the Menlo Park Veterans' Hospital. There, he often spent time talking to the patients, at times under the influence of the hallucinogenic drugs he'd taken as a volunteer for scientific experimentation. Kesey did not believe that these patients were insane, but rather that society had pushed them out because they did not fit the conventional ideas of how people were supposed to act and behave.

Moulin Rouge. This is a great musical that takes place in turn-of-the-century Paris of 1899. Ewan McGregor and Nicole Kidman lead the way through this often heartbreaking love triangle story.

Raging Bull. Robert De Niro gives an Oscar-winning performance in yet another brilliantly directed film by Martin Scorsese. Filmed in black and white, this is the true story of the boxer Jake Lamotta who could not escape his violent roots of the Bronx. Your great grandfather Bernie Allen has a small part as the comedian on stage at the Copacabana.

The Departed. For this film, Martin Scorsese finally wins a well-deserved overdue Academy Award for directing. This film's all-star cast turn in awesome performances led by Leonardo DiCaprio, Matt Damon, Jack Nicholson, Mark Wahlberg and Alec Baldwin.

The Wizard of Oz. This is classic Hollywood magic with the sweet voice of Judy Garland as Dorothy and a trio of old school Hollywood actors playing her three sidekicks. "Toto, I don't think we're in Kansas anymore."

300. A feast for the eyes, highlighting the battle of Thermopylae in 480 BC when Spartan warriors made a last stand against more than 100,000 in the Persian army. Gerard Butler gives a great performance as King Leonidas. "The world will know that free men stood against a tyrant, that few stood against many, and before this battle was over, even a God-king can bleed."

Legends of the Fall. An epic tale of three brothers living in the wilderness of the U. S. in the early 1900s. Brad Pitt gives a great performance and never looked prettier, along with great performances by Anthony Hopkins and Aidan Quinn.

Gandhi. Winner of eight Academy Awards, this is the biography of one of the great saints of the modern age with an incredible performance by Ben Kingsley and direction by Richard Attenborough.

Willy Wonka and the Chocolate Factory. This movie was an instant classic starring Gene Wilder as Willy Wonka with lessons for children and adults alike. "We are the music makers, and we are the dreamers of dreams."

The Princess Bride. An all-star cast keeps everyone laughing in this extremely funny and sweet tale of true love. I was 19 and fell instantly in love with Robin Wright. Billy Crystal is absolutely hysterical. "Have fun storming the castle, boys!"

The Graduate. A young and boyish Dustin Hoffman becomes a household name and is nominated for the Academy Award for Best Actor. He tries to fight off the advances of the sultry Ann Bancroft as Mrs. Robinson and his inner turmoil is palpable. The film is accompanied by one of the best soundtracks ever in film, highlighted by the songs of Simon and Garfunkel including the timeless blockbuster "Mrs. Robinson."

The Incredibles. Brad Bird writes and directs my favorite animated film. A family of super heroes in hiding saves the world by coming together as a team.

Seven Samurai. One of the greatest directors in film was a Japanese man named Akira Kurusawa. The great Toshiro Mifune stars in this film about a group of Samurai who come to the aid of a helpless town that is being terrorized by bandits. The American remake also became a huge hit, called *The Magnificent Seven.*

Harold and Maude. This is a dark comedy starring Ruth Gordon and Bud Cort. Young Harold is obsessed with death and finds friendship with Maude who is in her 70s. Grandpa Karl took me and your Uncle David to see this movie in a Ruth Gordon double feature along with the hysterical *Where's Poppa?*

It's a Mad, Mad, Mad, Mad World. One of the greatest comedic casts ever in a film are chased by Spencer Tracy and go crazy trying to find stolen money buried under the "big W."

The Producers. The master Mel Brooks writes and directs a masterpiece of comedy. Once again Gene Wilder gives a great comic performance along with the larger-than-life Zero Mostel. This original is much better than the remake and also has a brief appearance by your great grandfather Bernie Allen as one of the Hitler auditioners for the ridiculously titled show, *"Springtime for Hitler."* His only line is, "A little vooden boy."

The Godfather and *Godfather II*. Francis Ford Coppola's masterpieces based on the novel by Mario Puzo. These films may have the greatest casts of actors in history, lead by Marlon Brando, Robert Deniro, Robert Duvall, James Caan and Al Pacino. Until he was 13, Al Pacino went to grade school with your grandmother Judy in the South Bronx. She told me that everyone called him Sonny back then.

Hero. Jet Li stars in this incredibly visionary martial arts film that inspires with some of the most amazing sequences and visuals ever written for film.

Enter the Dragon. This movie stars the one and only Bruce Lee at his very best.

Life of Pi. Ang Lee directs a masterful film with imagery to fulfill the greatest imaginations. This is a spiritual film full of the mysteries of life and a boy's will to survive, stranded in a lifeboat with a Bengal tiger.

Kung Fu Hustle. This very funny comedy action film has incredible special effects and a wonderful message behind the story. My dear friend and karate sensei David Gonzalez recently wrote the following narrative that reflects the same message of the film: "Breathe in the gift of life. Breathe out a song of peace. The first level of martial arts is to learn how to destroy your opponents. The second level is to be able to subdue your opponents without hurting them. The highest level is to be able to change your opponent's heart thus spreading peace, compassion and love."

Film has always been a big part of my life, and it has always been my favorite art form. I hope that you find as many lessons in the films you choose to watch, and I will greatly look forward to watching some of my favorites with you someday soon. I will make the popcorn.

Oscar Wilde is famous for saying, "Life imitates art far more than *art imitates life*." Just like in life, I am sure that as we watch these great movies together, we will laugh many laughs and shed many tears.

Love always,
Dad

The Liberated Life

Jana
Ontario, Canada
June 2010

There is a way to live your life
that's happy every day.
There is a way to live your life
with joy in every way.

It demands resolve to rise above,
and asks from you your heartfelt love,
it takes some dedication,
and needs some meditation

to connect with spirit deep inside,
and from your self you cannot hide,
the light inside can shine so bright,
luminous to all in day or night.

When your heart is open and your mind is clear,
and you choose love instead of fear,
with gratitude and grace you cannot miss,
your life is free, your life is bliss.

—Adam Kleinberg

Excessive Happiness

Naia and Ananda
Wave Hill-Riverdale, the Bronx, N.Y.
June 2011

I am still determined to be cheerful and happy, in whatever situation I may be; for I have also learned from experience that the greater part of our happiness or misery depends upon our dispositions, and not upon our circumstances.

—Martha Washington

August 2011

Dear girls,

Over the course of the last couple of years, I have noticed a trend in the comments and compliments people give to you girls when we are out in public. It might be at a store, at a restaurant or at a playground where you are playing with their children. There are several similar things that parents tell me about you. They tell me you are beautiful. How nice! But more importantly, I love observing how very friendly you girls are and how you will say hello to everyone. Jana is always complimenting people on their shoes and dresses, and Naia has a very funny way of saying "Hallllooooo" to people. Ananda is just smiling and laughing all the time, and I do not find it ironic that her name literally means "bliss."

The other comment people often say to me is, "Your children are so happy." People everywhere go out of their way to tell me this. While these communications to me about your happiness are mostly congratulatory, they also seem to be tinted with a bit of astonishment. It is almost as if people can't understand or haven't seen very often the type of joy that radiates from you. You girls really are very happy. That is not to say you don't have your moments! You are human and you are young children, but you are very joyful kids.

I heard those words often enough and expressed in such a specific way, that it started to feel like your happiness was something not normal. It felt really weird. There is even a clinical disorder now that is called EHD or *Excessive Happiness Disorder*. The medical establishment wants you to think there is something wrong with you even if you are happy all the time!

Seriously?

People have a lot of distorted ideas about happiness. But I want you to remember that happiness can never be found on the outside, not in all the ways that people usually seek it. It cannot be found in food or champagne, sex or money, or anything outside of you. An author named John Bradshaw coined the expression "inner child." People often now talk about finding their inner child as a way to find happiness. Perhaps they should say *be* the inner child.

You three girls are shining examples of how to *be* happy. When I watch you run through the playground, go down a slide or jump into a pool, it is apparent there is nothing else on your mind. Like all children in their natural state, you are right here, present and in the moment. All the worries of the future and regrets of the past don't yet exist in your consciousness.

When you get older and the stresses of life start to weigh on you, remember that inside you are still the same beautiful, happy and joyful beings you always were. Remember back to when all you could think about was how you were going to jump in that puddle without me seeing you do it. Remember how you didn't care about the non-dairy ice cream dripping down your arm. Remember how you didn't have a care in the world. In honesty, you still don't have a care in the world and you never will. As Richard Carlson penned, "Don't sweat the small stuff, and it's all small stuff."

Remember that you are in control of your mind and where you put your attention. What you choose to think about is what you will create. Remember to choose happiness just like you did when you were little girls. Gandhi said, "A man is but the product of his thoughts; what he thinks, he becomes."

So my little darlings, continue to choose being happy! What could be a higher priority in your lives?

Love Always,
Dad

Part VI
Freedom

Jana
Santa Cruz, Calif.
July 2009

The Greatest Trip I've Ever Had

The Baths at Esalen, Big Sur, Calif.

Most men and women lead lives at the worst so painful, at the best so monotonous, poor and limited that the urge to escape, the longing to transcend themselves if only for a few moments, is and has always been one of the principal appetites of the soul.
        —Aldous Huxley (from *The Doors of Perception*)

My life has been long, and believing that life loves the liver of it, I have dared to try many things, sometimes trembling, but daring still.

        —Dr. Maya Angelou

March 2012

Dear girls,

On Labor Day weekend of 2009, while we were all living in Santa Cruz, your honorary Uncle D came to visit from New York. We will call him Uncle D to retain his anonymity and the "honorary" applies because he is not by blood your uncle but by brotherhood of the heart with me. He, your mother and I spent a weekend together at the Esalen Institute in Big Sur. Later, I wrote the poem "Ode to Three" that follows this letter. At the time, a poem was the only way I could express in words what I was feeling about the experience I'd had. The following narrative gives a more detailed account.

I tried psilocybin mushrooms for the first time in 2002 at the age of 34 while staying at a private villa on Ibiza, which is one of the Spanish Islands. Almost all of my trips since then have been at the Esalen Institute, although one was in Amsterdam (the only one at night and with peyote in addition to mushrooms), and one was at Harbin Hot Springs.

Because I have done a large amount of reading about the psychedelic experience, I put my trust in incredible authors like Dr. Timothy Leary, Dr. Gordon Wasson, Dr. Stanislov Grof, Peter Stafford, Ralph Metzner, Terence McKenna, Richard Evans Schultes, David Jay Brown, Huston Smith, Dr. John Lilly, Adam Gottlieb and Aldous Huxley. This list of revolutionary geniuses helped me preview what I would be experiencing, and therefore I had no fears about what might happen. I knew the psilocybin mushrooms were not toxic to the body, as is alcohol, cigarettes, prescription drugs, over-the-counter drugs and inhalants. Those toxic substances don't grow in nature, but mushrooms do.

I would like to make this important distinction, and make it perfectly clear: A drug is something made by man, and a plant is something made by nature. We shouldn't confuse the two by calling psychedelic plants "drugs," because they are not drugs, by definition.

They are natural substances, untouched by man. The Earth has given us a few special plants, and if we ingest them, they can help us to commune well with nature. That is not what drugs do!

By my second trip, I knew how to optimize and guard the sacred experience I was planning. I realized on every trip almost immediately that I was connecting to something greater than myself. This fungus was increasing my consciousness of the natural world and what lay beyond it, and decreasing my consciousness of the daily, material world of ego and body image.

After many years of studying the philosophies of the East, it was easy to see the similarities of the psychedelic experience and those experiences that came from practicing meditation and Buddhism. A great book that delves intelligently and visually into this similarity is called *Zig Zag Zen,* edited by Allan Hunt Badiner. This book declares itself to be "…the first serious inquiry into the moral, ethical, doctrinal and transcendental considerations created by the intersection of Buddhism and psychedelics." I think that says it all!

I treated every experience with great care following the sage advice of those many mentors listed previously. I have now had eight experiences, and none have been less than magnificent. The most entertaining, well-planned and superlative of these was over that Labor Day weekend in 2009.

Uncle D came to visit, and we planned a trip down the coast from Santa Cruz to Big Sur. We had reserved a private cabin at Esalen, and I had procured dried Mexican mushrooms, also known by one name as *stropharia cubensis.* I ground the dried mushrooms into a powder, which we would mix into fresh squeezed orange juice and drink in the morning on an empty stomach. This would optimize the effect and minimize the time for the active compounds to enter into our bloodstreams and into our brains.

The weather was clear and beautiful in Big Sur that day with the backdrop of mountains that climb to the crystal blue sky and crash spectacularly into the sea. Esalen is a natural paradise of the modern world. It is the perfect place to experience communion with nature. It is the perfect place to grow more conscious of our divine nature and the higher spiritual forces that are within us.

There are no electronics in the rooms at Esalen. There are no clocks, no computers, no TVs, no phones, no radios and no cell-phone reception. Nature is all around you. A large garden is the epicenter of the grounds. The ocean is within earshot. There are beautiful flowers everywhere. Monarch butterflies nest by the hundreds in bushes right outside your door. The mineral hot baths are built into the cliffs and sit high above the crashing waves of the mighty Pacific below. Sea lions flip their tales up at you; pelicans fly the coast, while bluebirds and finches are everywhere. Seasonally, you can see the migrating whales. The entire place is brimming with life.

After ingesting our mushrooms we spent our first hour or so in a shared meditation and inevitably began laughing a bit, which is reminiscent of a typical start with mushrooms. We expected our trip to last about eight hours. There was something poignant and funny that occurred during our affirmations in meditation when we were all saying, *Every cell of my being is filled with joy.* We all started laughing because for the moment, on our very happy way into deeper realms of consciousness, that statement was completely accurate.

We had a small bite to eat in the dining hall, so we would not come down starving after our trip. We then wandered into the garden between the ocean and the mountains. The garden has flowers everywhere, as well as lettuces, chickens and insects. Little sanctuaries of beauty fill this garden that feeds Esalen's visitors. The first few hours of a mushroom trip are typically the most hallucinatory or visual. Mushroom visuals tend towards rounded forms and images similar to nature. The colors of flowers, plants and the shape of mountains and clouds can be extremely beautiful. I couldn't think of a more perfect place to be than Esalen on a day full of brilliant California coastal sunshine.

After an hour or two in the garden, we all had grown peaceful from the natural beauty that surrounded us, and it was time to turn our energies toward inner-space. We all needed to go enjoy the inner experience, so it was nice to have a quiet and peaceful room with three beds to return to out of the sun. It felt great to drink some water. The only thing that my stomach seems to let me ingest during a mushroom trip is water. It is not that I feel sick in any way; it is that the mushrooms seem to turn off my lower chakras and leave me with no appetite whatsoever for food or sex. All energies are directed toward the higher chakras, which produce a heightened state of empathy, compassion and communion with life and the divine. All the guards are down and a person can just be who they are with no pretense and no ego. Your mother experienced her first mushroom trip on an earlier visit to Esalen, and I watched her grow free for a short time from the great ego masquerade.

Once we returned from the garden, we were all peaking in our experience. The cabin's wood walls had visible knots that were darker than the other areas. These dark knots served as a focal point for me to see the wood as "coming to life." In our conversations that night, we all three realized we had this same visual observation. I'd had the same visuals in my previous psychedelic experiences. Everything seems to be more alive while on mushrooms, as if everything were breathing. You can witness the expansion and contraction of it all, like a divine dance. The beauty in everything seems to shine from within, and you are saturated with an understanding of the universe that is not possible to put into words.

Some of the inner visuals I had on this particular trip were of native temples and spirits. I was communing with beings from elsewhere. This was not the first time I had this type of experience on psilocybin mushrooms. The mushroom allows for an alternate reality, one that allows a significant opening of your being. If we are normally able to commune with and observe three dimensions, the mushroom allows a communion and observation with many more.

Uncle D is also a chiropractor and was adjusting my spine all through the morning and afternoon, and I was adjusting him and your mother just as often. We cleared all of our nerve systems of any interference to heighten the spiritual experience we were having. All in all, from the night before to the end of our trip, each of us probably got adjusted seven or eight times. I could feel my spine start to un-torque and could feel an unraveling of its protective coverings. I could feel my whole body moving into a state of clarity and centered relaxation. I used to hear Dr. Dick Santo lecture to large groups that chiropractic adjustments connect *man the spiritual* with *man the physical*. God rest his beautiful soul. What could be more important than clearing the nerve system to heighten a sacramental and transcendental experience?

Your mother contributed to our healing in a profound way as well. At some point she informed us that she was channeling a benevolent energy or spirit. While Uncle D and I lay on our backs with eyes closed on parallel beds, your mother did some energy work on us. In conversations after our trip, he and I agreed that the same thing was done and the reaction was the same. Your mother put one hand on my lower belly and one finger on my forehead at the location of the third eye, and said, "A gift for the healers." All at once, I felt a wave of grace come over me. My dedication to help others in life was instantly understood, and I felt an overwhelming psychological and emotional comfort.

There was a tremendous amount of universal love and compassion flowing through your mother that day, and so her healing energy caused the same reaction in both Uncle D and I. Uncontrollable laughter mixed with tears flowing out of us. We also experienced a dissipation of energy from our bodies, almost like shivering and shaking without being cold. Once that twisted energy left our bodies, in its place, there was something calm, clear and balanced—something *whole*.

After an hour or so of this responsive release, we were all very clear, emotionally wide open and still feeling great effects from the mushrooms. We finally made our way outside of our cabin again, this time to take another walk through the garden. The southern side of Esalen where we were at the moment was starting to lose visibility of the sunset, and the light was starting to fade. All the footlights that dotted the paths were beginning to glow as we slowly made our way to the northern side of the property.

The path descends to a wooden bridge that crosses a waterfall that empties into the Pacific Ocean. Sitting over that waterfall is a round, wooden house for silent meditation. At the top of the hill, as we started our descent along the path and caught a glimpse of the sunset on the north side, your Uncle D turned to me and said, "Is this the path to heaven?" He really meant it, and his eyes were filled with a pure innocence as he spoke.

We all started to laugh with joy all the way to the other side of the grounds, and there witnessed the full and unobstructed view of the grandest Pacific coast sunset. It was a brick red, orange, pink and yellow sunset that just kept getting more and more colorful as the minutes went by. In that moment, we were all hit by the glory of that sunset, and I felt as if my eyes could see 360 degrees around my whole head. It was as if the sunset were a painting that had been put onto a vast canvas of sky by my very soul.

We all began to weep at the same time, overwhelmed by the beauty we were witnessing. I've thought many times that this one experience, this one day, if others could experience it as we did, would change even the most apathetic person. I thought if more people had experiences like the one we were having, there would be a lot more peace and non-violence on Earth. I felt a deep gratitude for life that only the greatest of poets could ever express with pen to paper. In that moment I was the embodiment of light, love, peace, joy, grace, abundance, wisdom and gratitude.

Your mother had found a wooden rocking chair on the grass to sit in, and told us that she was sitting with the spirit of an old, wise woman. I don't doubt it for a second. We watched the sun slowly melt into the ocean. We watched the sky in metamorphosis every few minutes and then watched the brilliance slowly fade into the night. Twilight appeared and the first brightest stars could be seen in the dark blue night sky, far above the full color spectrum of the horizon.

We made our way back to our cabin and finally had the first pangs of something resembling hunger. I had packed some amazing fruit for us from the Santa Cruz farmers' market. I had sweet melons, peaches, plums, pluots and cherries, most from Frog Hollow Farms. There is nothing like sweet fresh fruit at the end of a mushroom trip. It was probably some of the finest organic fruit on the planet. It is wonderful to be provided such delicacies from Mother Earth when you are in such a deep state of gratitude.

As the moon began to show itself over the ocean, we made our way from our cabin down the hill to the sulphur-rich hot baths. The baths are stone and built into the side of the cliff about 50 feet above the ocean. They are certainly one of the most special components of Esalen. Nudity is optional at the baths, and I have never bothered to wear any clothes. It is very liberating to be nude in a semi-public place where the visitors are sophisticated and Bohemian enough to not care if they catch a glimpse of genitalia.

We soaked in the baths for hours, experiencing a deep physical state of relaxation. The baths at Esalen also have showers with giant sliding glass doors that open to the ocean. You can't help but notice the architecture, the dim lighting, the shapes, the art and the nature surrounding you. Words do not do the experience of Esalen justice. Esalen has been an institute for the human potential movement for 50 years now. I highly recommend Jeffrey J. Kripal's book entitled *Esalen: America and the Religion of No Religion*.

I have visited baths both at Esalen and at Harbin Hot Springs. Harbin is also an incredible place and at Harbin the hot bath is *very* hot. There is also a cold pool that is filled by water flowing in directly from the nearby mountain stream. I have done alternating hot-cold baths there for several hours and relieved my body and mind of every ounce of stress. Nudity is also optional at Harbin. Your mother and I had one mushroom trip there in 2008 shortly after the twins were born. We lay naked together on a blanket in the grass under the shade of a tree, like Adam and Eve in the Garden of Eden.

After bathing in the Esalen tubs, we three made our way back to our cabin for some sleep. The sulphur in the baths tends to completely clear out the sinuses, allowing for a high sensitivity to the sense of smell. Some of my favorite smells in life happen along the moonlit walk up the hill from the baths at Esalen. Besides the scent of the ocean and the wildflowers, the sweet smell of eucalyptus is enough to stop me in my tracks, make me close my eyes and take several deep breaths. When I open my eyes again on that hill and look around, I find it hard to conceive where I am, being so totally overwhelmed by beauty. No matter where I may be, in my mind's eye I can always imagine and feel myself standing on that hill with my face glowing in the moonlight and the gentle winds of the Pacific washing over me.

We stopped at the dining hall for some late-night snacks. All of us were in a very wonderful place, contemplating and discussing the experiences of our day. I can't imagine it is a day that any of us will soon forget. Our experience had helped us to grow more conscious of our divine nature with the help of the *entheogens* we had ingested.

Wikipedia defines an *entheogen* as "God inside us," and further refers to an entheogen as "a psychoactive substance used in a religious, shamanic or spiritual context." Plants like peyote, ayahuasca and psilocybin mushrooms are considered entheogenic, which means they are capable of generating the divine within. I have always tried to prepare and guide my experiences to be sacred. But not everyone takes this approach. While living in Amsterdam, I had two friends tell me they ate some mushrooms and then went to see *Jurassic Park III*. They did not have a single clue as to the potential of what they were doing. What they chose for their psychedelic experience was like listening to heavy metal music on an iPod while being surrounded by a live orchestra at the symphony.

Wikipedia goes on to say that "Entheogens can supplement many diverse practices for healing, transcendence and revelation, including meditation, psychonautics, art projects and psychedelic therapy. More broadly, the term *entheogen* is used to refer to any psychoactive substances when used for their religious or spiritual effects, whether or not in a formal religious or traditional structure. This terminology is often chosen to contrast with recreational use of the same substances."

It is not difficult to understand the common experience that has been written about and studied involving psilocybin mushrooms if you look in the right places. Not surprisingly, operating out of Santa Cruz, California, the Multidisciplinary Association for Psychedelic Studies (MAPS) is a great group to look to for more information and to learn what is currently being studied for therapeutic and spiritual purposes. Another great source online is Erowid.org. On their homepage it states the site's purpose as: "...documenting the complex relationship between humans and psycho-actives."

I am not writing here to condone the use of mushrooms or any other plant for that matter. What I wanted to accomplish by writing this to you was to give you an honest and poetic account of a profound experience in my life. When you girls are adults and are emotionally developed enough, you may want to create your own plant-based entheogenic experiences to explore the sacred inner journey that these substances offer. Know that I will always be there to guide you with love and non-judgment. My hope is to help you experience what you want to in the safest, most effective way and to help you enrich your experience as much as possible.

My spiritual beliefs, like most Eastern traditions, are centered on the experiential rather than on dogma and tradition. I hope that at a young age you girls choose an Eastern path instead of the typical tradition of blind faith that most Western religions follow. Terence

McKenna said, "If the words 'life, liberty, and the pursuit of happiness' don't include the right to experiment with your own consciousness, then the Declaration of Independence isn't worth the hemp it was written on."

I am here to guide you, and when the day comes that I have left this Earth, you can read the pages of this book and fill your hearts with the eternal love that I will always have for each of you girls. Nothing will ever change that, not the passing of time or even death. Death is only of the body. These special plants have helped me peel back the veil of my consciousness to see the divine energy that is alive in everything. It is a great comfort to know from my own experience that the divine energy we share will always keep us connected.

Love always,
Always,
Dad

Naia and Ananda
Riverdale, the Bronx, N.Y.
August 2011

Ode to Three

Three
The Magik Number,
Three days, Three Healers

Gave gifts of healing on sacred land
Found boundless empathy within their heart
Mother Earth's wisdom within their mind
Wept with joy, wept with joy

Floated though flower gardens into the forest
Down the glowing trail and over the bridge
Became one with the sunset, body left behind
Communing with sprits from other worlds
The ocean reflecting
The sky on fire, sky on fire

Bathed by the moon in mineral pools
Hot and cold cathartic cleanse
Healers' burden washed away
The ocean breeze-kisses caressing our body
Alignment, alignment

Daredevil finds the path to Heaven
White Sorceress released from heavy yoke
Alchemist shares his visions of love
Three became One with deep gratitude
For all, for all

—Adam Kleinberg

Death Is Just a Part of Life

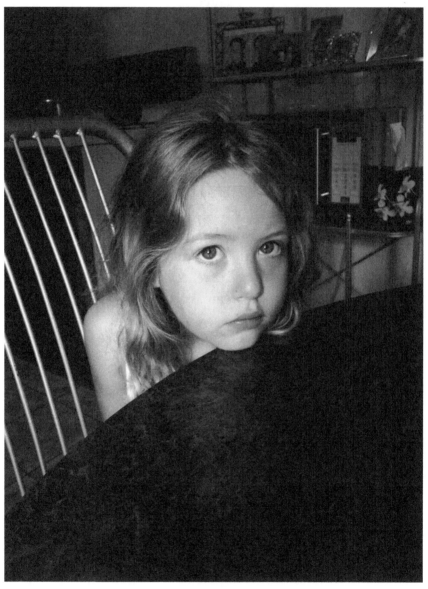

Jana in Grandma Judy's kitchen
July 2011

It's not that I'm afraid to die, I just don't want to be there when it happens.

—Woody Allen

February 2012

Dear girls,

Sometimes it is hard to remember that we have nothing to fear. More than 150,000 people die every day. So why then does it come as such a shock when someone we know passes on? Do not fear death. Let it have no power over you. We are all sure to perish, so why not instead embrace life and live it? Every person dies, but not every person really lives. Live your life fearlessly and with passion!

Shiva is the Hindu God known as the Destroyer or Transformer. Shiva will visit us all. We all must return to ashes. When someone passes it is a sad day for most, but it doesn't have to be. Most humans somehow think that they will live in their bodies forever. Most don't think about death. They rarely contemplate their own demise. I believe that death is just a doorway, a transmutation of energy.

It is an amazing thing to let go of fear and to find grace. Imagine yourself a leaf caught up in a storm's wind, being blown about with whimsy and having no resistance to where you are taken. Allow your life to take you where it may, and try to find acceptance and joy for the path regardless of the destination.

I think it is our individual personalities that we are afraid of losing, more than we fear losing our bodies. That is the ego. All the saints and sages have something to say about that pesky little ego of ours. There is a blissful freedom that can come from detaching from the body and the physical, and connecting with spirit and one's true essence. Your soul is immortal. Your body is the soul's divine temple.

You have the ability to be grateful! Right now! This moment! You can be grateful regardless of your circumstances if you choose to be. Gandhi did it. Many enlightened ones have done it. Gandhi said, "What is possible for one is possible for all." When you are able to guide the thoughts of your mind, you are then the captain of your own ship, and you can stay on course toward the North Star. Staying on course means not allowing your thoughts to control you but rather you controlling them.

When you are grateful, death doesn't matter. When you know something divine is within you and within everything else, then death is meaningless. The term *maya* means "illusion" and was derived from the Sanskrit. You just have to be able to open up your eyes from this illusion to see all the love that always surrounds you. Remember that you are never alone.

Death will eventually visit me, too, although like most people I hate to admit it. But death could not stop me from sending waves of love directly into your hearts even from the edges of the universe. Death will not affect the love I have for you. It is now, it is infinite, and it is always. If you girls search deep inside yourselves, even many decades after I am gone, you will still be able to feel my love as deeply as the day I held you for the first time.

The Chilean poet Pablo Neruda wrote one of my favorite poems which was addressed to his wife. Although you are my daughters, his words still apply.

Sonnet LXXXIX

When I die, I want your hands on my eyes:
I want the light and the wheat of your beloved hands
to pass their freshness over me once more,
I want to feel the softness that changed my destiny.
I want you to live while I wait for you, asleep.
I want your ears still to hear the wind; I want you
to sniff the sea's aroma that we loved together,
to continue to walk on the sand we walk on.

I want what I love to continue to live,
and you whom I love and sang above everything else
to continue to flourish, full-flowered,
So that you can reach everything my love directs you to,
so that my shadow can travel along in your hair,
so that everything can learn the reason for my song.

Love Always,
From here and the great beyond,
Dad

Naia, Jana and Ananda
Wave Hill-Riverdale, the Bronx, N.Y.
June 2011

Shiva

Oh Shiva, great Destroyer,
Please free me from my life.
Take me back to nothingness
That I have always been.

Free me from my body
And all its tensions twisting,
Free me from my tortured mind
And all its endless thinking,

Free me from my obligations
Pain, and petty matters,
Free me from my heart that aches
My empathy, and compassion.

Let me soar along the wind
With wings of spirit free,
Let me sit inside a star
Its fire alight in me,

Let me be the shadow
Of my children, oh so fair,
Let me be the sweet smell
Of the Lilac in their hair,

Let me float with grace
On oceans of time
Bring me back to spirit,
Back to the source, the One.

Aum Nama Shivaya
Aum Nama Shivaya
Aum Nama Shivaya
Oh, Shiva please come.

—Adam Kleinberg

Shine Your Love on the World

Jana
Riverdale, the Bronx, N.Y.
June 2011

Yesterday I was clever, so I wanted to change the world.
Today I am wise, so I am changing myself.

—Rumi

November 2012

Dear Jana, Naia and Ananda,

Writing this book has been an amazing labor of love. I took great care to pay attention to every detail. It took several hours on occasion to find just the right quote, phrase, study, picture or bit of information that I felt I needed in order to make this book as special as possible for you. I hope that in reading it you have paid attention and found joy in these details as well.

I also hope you find the poems with as many lessons and love as the rest of the book. They seemed to flow through me with amazing ease. Although this entry is the last letter written to you in this book, there are two more entries for you to read. I wanted to share what is currently one of my most passionate endeavors with you girls and with all other "wellness-minded" readers. Read about it in the Afterword, beginning with *An Open Letter to Morgan Spurlock* and followed by *Summer Camp: The Shine Your Light Project*. I hope it will be a project you take part in someday.

I have learned so much along the way; one does indeed teach what one needs to learn. There are many lessons, concepts and experiences that I have tried to share and reveal to you in the pages I have written. Of all the lessons that I may try to teach you in the time we have left together on this Earth, this simple letter may include the most important one, which is also the title I gave to this book, and that is to *shine your love on the world.*

I was surprised to see in my searches for a book title that *Shine Your Love on the World* had not been used to date. It has always been the title of this book from the moment I conceived it and before any writing was begun. I am sincerely delighted that I chose a title from my heart that is still something original. I think it is important for you to know why I wrote a book to you three girls with that title, and what those words mean to me.

I believe that you girls have the ability to live your lives centered in and flowing in a state of love. I believe that you can project that love outward to overcome the negative circumstances and influences that lie ahead of you. "Shine your love on the world," means to realize your internal state of abundance, compassion, joy, gratitude and peace. It means to project that internal state onto everything you come across and infuse that attitude into everything you do. I will do everything in my power to help you to create that internal state.

Deep in the roots of the wisdom traditions of the world is a mystical power you and anyone can acquire through right thought and right action. This power allows you to be in a state of happiness or bliss regardless of your surroundings or life circumstances. When you can summon this internal power to create and project love from within, you can then project that love outward onto the world around oneself.

In the *Bhagavad Gita*, which is a 5,000-year-old Hindu scripture, the warrior Arjuna and Lord Krishna remain calm on the battlefield and in deep conversation in the middle of a war that is raging relentlessly around them. This represents internal peace in the face of external turmoil. We cannot escape the turmoil of the world, but we can learn to keep control over our minds and be the peaceful center of a tumultuous cyclone.

I have already been a witness to you girls bringing much joy into the world around you wherever life takes us. It is so much fun and so rewarding to watch you consistently interact with strangers in the most open and loving ways. People

often express so much gratitude just to have crossed paths with you. You always have big beautiful smiles for everyone and your laughter is absolutely contagious.

You are courteous, gentle and consistently complimenting others. You also often express a compassionate wisdom that flows from the innocence of youth. I have not witnessed any of you with any real malice or vindictiveness, although like most siblings you can get under each other's skin from time to time.

I hope to help you understand your true nature as spiritual beings having a human experience, and for you to be able to identify with yourselves as divine beings of light. You represent everything that is right and beautiful about life. This concept of your true nature is what I hope to pass onto you girls. I hope that no matter what happens in your life, no matter how bleak things may seem, you can call upon the infinite spirit within you to overcome any challenge.

You will certainly not always have things go the way you want them to, but it will be your attitude and perception that will decide how you are affected by those challenges and what the future will hold for you. If I can help you to understand that you are creating your own reality from within, and I get to witness you begin to live your lives balanced in this one universal truth, then I will be able to leave my body behind with an eternal smile on my face.

A day will come that I am no longer here to hold your hand along the way but know this; my love for you is perennial, it is something infinite. As long as I am here in body my energy belongs to you. When you can no longer feel the warmth of my hugs, my spirit will still reside in your heart, and you will be able to call on me for guidance. Tolstoy understood this when he wrote a book titled *The Kingdom of God Lies Within You*, borrowing the words from the Bible spoken by Jesus.

In the silent stillness, you will continue to feel me, you will continue to hear me, and you will continue to see me pointing you toward the love that lies within you always. Remember there is never anything to fear. Remember that there is never anything to lose. You are already complete.

To my three angels, Jana Aum, Naia Aum and Ananda Aum,
All my love and blessings,
Always and forever,
Dad

Afterword
A Proposal for the
Wellness–minded

Jana, Ananda and Naia
Ontario, Canada
October 2011

An Open Letter to Morgan Spurlock

Naia, Jana and Ananda
Kingston Ontario, Canada
December 2012

There is nothing more powerful than an idea whose time has come.

—Victor Hugo

November 2012
Mr. Morgan Spurlock
New York, NY

Dear Morgan,

Although we have never met, I have been chasing you for the last several years, well, mostly in my mind. I have been in touch periodically with many of your staff, including two personal assistants, and while in New York I made a couple of impromptu visits to your film production company that you founded in 2004, Warrior Poets, and chatted with your former assistant Sarah. Your people were very supportive and encouraging, but when all is said and done you are a hard man to get to.

I have at times been one crazed moment away from a perpetual fast in front of your office building, carrying a sign that reads *Meet with me Morgan, don't let me starve to death, I've got three daughters!* That might sound crazy because it is true, but a less radical head prevailed, and I figured I might be better able to get your attention if this letter was in my book. I want my daughters to learn that perseverance is paramount in life.

I am writing to you today on behalf of our children. Your son Laken is the same age as my eldest daughter Jana, and my twins Naia and Ananda are two years younger. I am intent on doing all I can to create a better world for them all. I know you probably have a ton of projects on your plate, but the one I am proposing is different. This one really is special, as its focus is on inspiring and empowering children to choose wellness-based approaches to life. For several years now I have been driven to tears and near madness staring at my vision board, specifically at the ingenious and idiotic picture of you with French fries overstuffed into your mouth. I, too, am a warrior poet. I hope that you are deeply drawn to my project and will want to be a part of the creation of the documentary series I am proposing, *Summer Camp: The Shine Your Light Project.*

Your film *Super-Size Me* is one of the main inspirations for this project. When I saw your film, as disgusted as I was by your ordeal, you became an instant hero to me. No one can deny that you are a clever man! When I was creating this project I thought to myself over and over, *If this guy can try to change the world by showing how sick he can make himself, why can't we show people how we can make a group of kids optimally healthy at a pivotal age in their lives?*

My intention is to inspire health and habit transformation for children on the largest scale possible. I believe with all my heart and soul that this project will help to ignite a new type of revolution for our children into the wellness paradigm that is so desperately needed. We can help millions of children have a profound change in their perception and health. Please feel my passion and take the short time out of your busy schedule to read the following proposal and supporting document. It's only seven pages!

I would like to share my vision with you for the worthiest of causes: the physical health and mental freedom of our children. No more preaching to the choir, no more focus on the darkness. Let's help usher in a new age of light for your child, my children and all of the infinitely beautiful children in the world.

Love and blessings,
Dr. Adam Kleinberg

A Proposal for Summer Camp: The *Shine Your Light* Project

There is strength, wisdom and courage already inside you.

—Dad
(inspired by the lyrics of India Arie.)

Jana
Ontario, Canada
October 2012

Introduction

It has been evident for some time now that there is a constant and growing epidemic of illness among the youth of America and the Western world. Chronic illnesses that are considered to be lifestyle based, such as obesity, heart disease, type 2 diabetes. Countless other conditions, including childhood cancer, autism, depression and asthma, are at pandemic levels and threaten to escalate exponentially without a drastic change to the habits of the majority of America's youth.

Along with the exponential growth of technology and the ease of information gathering and processing, the American way of life has pervaded countries and cultures all over the world. The results of these cultural lifestyle changes show alarming and catastrophic results to the health of modern society. Most unfortunate are our children who are subjected to the habits heralded by the pop culture and the multi-national corporate advertising machine that poisons the minds of human beings for profit.

The human race continually has a close eye on America and our culture of convenience, materialism, entertainment and instant gratification. We have been covertly misled into a mindset that fosters disease of the body, the mind and even the soul. However, more and more people are beginning to believe and understand that a great paradigm shift is currently occurring and is rapidly building momentum.

Summer Camp: The Shine Your Light Project will have an epic inspirational impact on the youth of America and the youth of the world. As a documentary series, *Summer Camp* will deliver a powerful message with an authoritative, funny and enlightening message to the world in the most rapid, practical and humorous way possible. It will illustrate the true potential of an integral and proactive wellness approach not only for physical health but for emotional and spiritual health as well.

The Project

Our project will take place in California with participants potentially chosen from the greater Los Angeles area. The summer camp will last eight weeks and the activities will integrate five common wellness practices: yoga, meditation, chiropractic, fitness and diet (mostly raw and totally vegan) into a synergistic program. Other wellness practices will be introduced as well, including massage, floatation tanks and *qi gong*. Teaching participants how to grow their own food and lessons on ecology will also be a focal point of a wellness program and philosophy.

Five male and five female high school freshmen and/or sophomores will be chosen for scholarship to our camp through submission of a one-page essay and three-minute video expressing why they want to attend our camp and be a part of our project. The interview phase will serve as pre-camp footage for the documentary. Two counselors will be assigned to each of the male and female groups. Counselors and camp leaders will also follow the complete program. All participants who complete the camp will be filmed for post-camp footage and supported for a minimum of one semester with biweekly support group meetings with their families.

Our participants will represent a cross section of races, economic classes and educational structures. This will not be some glorified fat camp. There are several key motivators with equal significance for participants to join our project, including weight loss, chronic physical illness, confidence building and increased athletic performance. The central purpose of this project is to share the experiences of our kids, and to transparently and clearly link their amazing changes to our integral program and a natural setting. We aim to show radical results in health, personality and performance, and we will choose a spectrum of participants from the "couch potato" to the elite athlete.

Participants will be monitored through initial and follow-up medical evaluations, chiropractic evaluations and subjective lifestyle questionnaires. No outside food or beverages, reading or entertainment material will be allowed. All electronic devices will be prohibited at our camp, although limited Internet access and telephone privileges will be permitted. Our website will have running footage showing the progress of all the campers and will be the point of contact for friends and family of our participants. Our website will be documenting messages of support and encouragement from viewers all over the country and potentially the world from sites like YouTube, Facebook, Instagram and Twitter, which will additionally serve to market and promote the project.

Our campers will undergo a seven-day a week program with Saturday serving as our day of rest and rebuilding. A typical day at camp will be as follows:

6:00   Wake, shower, juice, supplementation
6:30   Morning meditation
7:15   Morning yoga
8:15   Breakfast
9:00   Classroom instruction
11:00   Fitness
12:00   Lunch
1:00   Free time
2:30   Sport instruction, chiropractic adjustments, leisure time
4:30   Afternoon meditation
5:00   Daily wrap
5:30   Dinner
7:00   Nature walk
8:00   Group discussion and support
8:30   Campfire and free time
10:00   Lights out

We will incorporate several field trips over the summer to raise the awareness of the best of a wellness-based lifestyle. Potential California field trips will include:

1. Raw and vegan restaurants, such as Cafe Gratitude and Millennium in San Francisco, and Planet Raw in Los Angeles.

2. Centers for human potential and well being including the

Esalen Institute in Big Sur and the Chopra Center for Well Being in San Diego.

3. A sporting event, including a practice day at a U.S. Golf or Tennis Championship.

Other events planned for the camp are movie nights, motivational guests, a mid-term parents' weekend, an educational symposium and a benefit concert finale.

The other major and critical component of this project is our plan to petition major sports figures, musicians and entertainment personalities to offer personal messages that advocate both the wellness practices of our program as well as the effect of those practices on their own lives. Because teenagers typically idolize people from these endeavors, it will serve as an additional compelling and entertaining part of the film. The fame factor will bring our project a wide audience demographic, including children, where other projects have failed and have only been able to "preach to the choir."

The list of figures who advocate at least part of our program include: Casey Affleck, Carol Alt, Lance Armstrong, David Beckham, Orlando Bloom, Kate Bosworth, Brandon Boyd, Brandy, Neve Campbell, Bill Clinton, Chelsea Clinton, Cheryl Crow, Ellen DeGeneres, Portia De Rossi, Prince Fielder, Danny Glover, Tony Gonzalez, Ginnifer Goodwin, Heather Graham, Laird Hamilton, Ben Harper, Woody Harrelson, Josh Hartnett, Evander Holyfield, Phil Jackson, Jack Johnson, Donna Karen, Anthony Kiedis, Tia Leoni, Carl Lewis, Jared Leto, David Lynch, Madonna, Tobey Maguire, Sir Paul McCartney, Moby, Lea Michele, Joe Montana, Demi Moore, Edwin Moses, Alonzo Mourning, Jason Mraz, Mike Myers, Dan O'Brien, Robert Parish, Joaquin Phoenix, Brad Pitt, Jeremy Piven, Natalie Portman, Jerry Rice, Anthony Robbins, Aaron Rodgers, John Sally, Carlos Santana, Alicia Silverstone, Russell Simmons, Emmitt Smith, Morgan Spurlock, Ringo Starr, Gwen Stefani, Sting, John Stockton,

Christy Turlington, Shania Twain, Eddie Vedder, Montel Williams, Reese Witherspoon, Tiger Woods, Stevie Wonder and many others. I realize this is a grandiose list, but big-name participation will be indispensible to grab the attention of our children.

Visits to the camp from a portion of these figures and short videos or interviews from a larger portion will be integrated into the project. Musicians will participate in the benefit concert finale to raise money to support a new non-profit organization called The Shine Your Light Foundation. Its purpose will be to teach habit and health transformation to children, and to fund the camp into a permanent program five times per year for adults and children alike.

The educational guests for our project will be utilized to bring expertise of a specific subject to help inspire our participants and educate our audience. Speakers such as Carol Alt, Dr. Deepak Chopra, Dr. Gabriel Cousens, Dr. Jason Deitch, Dr. Joe Dispenza, Dr. Masaru Emoto, Dr. Patrick Gentempo, Lee Holden, Michael Hutchison, Dean Kamen, Dr. Bruce Lipton, Lynne McTaggert, Dan Millman, Dr. Tim O'Shea, Anthony Robbins, John Robbins, Eric Schloesser, Dr. Liam Schubel, Morgan Spurlock, Christy Turlington, Ken Wilber and Marianne Williamson could lend immeasurable credibility to the underlying philosophies and science our project is based on.

The main goal is the creation of a project that is as entertaining as it is informative and enlightening. The use of montage and first-person narration will be fundamental tools utilized. Music from artists like Stevie Wonder, Red Hot Chili Peppers, Richie Havens and Eddie Vedder will comment effectually on the project's philosophies.

Corporate sponsorships will be created for support, and we will profile like-minded companies whose specific products we will utilize for the project. This project has universal appeal to a wide audience demographic due to its inspirational nature and all-star contributors. Great change and rapid development over a relatively short period of time is a subject matter that typically fascinates the viewer. Just think of *Super Size Me* or *The Biggest Loser*.

It is time we launch a unified message of wellness to our children. Films such as *Super Size Me*, *Doctored*, *Forks over Knives*, *Food Fight*, *Food Inc.*, *Enlighten Up*, Jeremy Piven's *Journey of a Lifetime*, David Lynch's *Meditation, Creativity, Peace* and *Simply Raw: Reversing Diabetes in 30 Days* have all been part of the inspiration for me to create this project.

This project is entertaining, compelling and will create dramatic conflict, challenging people to think. It can be an effective venue for many like-minded people to give a universal message to our children. With little individual effort, a multitude of people of fame and knowledge will come together with a common message and a common mission. They will show their support to a group of teenage kids who are sacrificing a carefree childhood summer to learn about a new way of life, to lead by example and who will in turn inspire a generation of sick and misled children into a brighter and healthier future. This project artistically represents a great hope and seeks to break down the walls of psychological oppression systematically broadcast to our kids through advertisements. This is THE PROJECT that can make wellness "cool" to masses of young people.

As Albert Einstein once said, "No problem can be solved from the same level of consciousness that created it." The philosophies of this project represent a message that is central to me, one that I cannot exist without. This is a story that absolutely must be told. These are the facts that must not stay hidden. The future of our children greatly depends on it. (Please read the Supplemental Summary for supporting documentation and statistics in the Appendix).

Appendix

1. Supplemental Summary for *Summer Camp: The Shine Your Light Project*

2. My Favorite Musicians, extended list- (from the letter Music Makes the World Go Round)

Ananda
Central Park, New York City
August 2011

1. Supplemental Summary for Summer Camp: The Shine Your Light Project

The combination of two key factors drives this documentary project toward a wide and potentially large audience demographic. These key factors are America's outdated approach to children's poor overall health habits and a collaboration of outspoken and passionate icons who will initiate a unified manifesto. The combined presentation of these two factors will be too compelling, entertaining and virtuous to be ignored by the masses.

People in our country and abroad, as well as the corporate world, are hungry for change and ready for a larger and stronger paradigm shift in the area of health. It is as obvious as Wal-Mart aspiring to become the largest retailer of organics. If people as different as Mike Tyson to Chelsea Clinton, Bill Clinton, Natalie Portman and Sanjay Gupta are condoning veganism, Eddie Vedder, Paul McCartney and David Lynch are collaborating to promote meditation, and Jerry Rice and Tiger Woods are singing the praises of chiropractic care, then the time for this project is now!

The United States represents 4% of the world's population. We consume 50% of the world's drugs and we now rank 29th for infant mortality. The CDC states, *"Infant mortality is one of the most important indicators of the health of a nation."* In addition diseases with dire consequences besiege our youth.

The last two decades have shown an exponential rise in autism, childhood cancer, childhood diabetes, childhood asthma and childhood obesity, among others. Current federally funded studies have revealed that 1 percent of all children in the USA have an autism spectrum disorder.

According to the Asthma and Allergy Foundation of America, asthma is the most common chronic disease of childhood, and in the United States, it is estimated that nearly 5 million children under age 18 have asthma. This is nearly 2% of the entire population of our country.

According to the National Conference of State Legislatures from a population of 300 million, 66 million Americans are overweight or obese. Over the past three decades, obesity rates have nearly tripled for children ages 2 to 5 (from 5% to 14%), more than tripled for youth ages 12 to 19 (from 5% to 17%) and more than quadrupled for children ages 6 to 11 (from 4% to 19%.) Currently, approximately 12 million children and adolescents are obese, and almost 30% do not exercise three or more days per week. Being overweight puts children and teenagers at greater risk for developing Type 2 diabetes, risk factors for heart disease at an earlier age, and other health conditions including asthma, sleep apnea and psychosocial effects such as decreased self-esteem. In one large study, 61% of overweight 5- to 10-year-olds already had at least one risk factor for heart disease, and 26 percent had two or more risk factors!

The obesity epidemic has led to an exponential increase in Type 2 diabetes in children. In 1992, it was rare for most pediatric centers to have any patients with Type 2 diabetes and by 1999, it accounted for 8–45% of new cases depending on geographic location. The current thought patterns and current paradigms are failing with miserable results and dire consequences.

Through habit transformation, the vast majority of disease and misery could be avoided. It is becoming more and more obvious and scientifically understood that lifestyle plays the greatest influence on one's own health. The gene theory and the outdated paradigm of believing that one is trapped into a genetic expression of disease are quickly crumbling upon incomplete Newtonian foundations. Dr. Joe Dispenza, who is featured in the film *What the Bleep Do We Know* and is the author of the books *Evolve Your Brain* and *Breaking the Habit of Being Yourself*, and Dr. Bruce Lipton, who is featured in the film *The Living Matrix* and is the author of the books *The Biology of Belief* and *Spontaneous Evolution*, are among the scientists proving the common assumption that genes rule our health to be false. Both have expressed strong support of this documentary project.

There are also many athletes who are open and passionate advocates of the wellness practices that have helped them achieve peak performance. Carl Lewis is outspoken that the peak of his career at age 30, which accompanied many Olympic gold medals, was manifested in large part due to his adherence to a vegan diet. The great hurdler Edwin Moses, Joe Namath, Martina Navratilova, Prince Fielder and Bill Walton (who also practices meditation) are vegetarians. Dave Scott holds the record for most Iron Man World Championship victories ever. Scott won six of them, all while vegetarian. He even came out of retirement at 40 to compete again, and took second place. Dr. Gabriel Cousens' documentary *Simply Raw, Reversing Diabetes in 30 Days* is one of the most inspiring films and will help implode many of the myths that still have power over the health decisions of most Americans. One man with insulin-dependent Type 2 diabetes is taken off 19 medications and insulin, and achieves normal blood sugar levels within weeks on a raw vegan diet.

Tiger Woods stated in his first interview after his scandal that he had quit his regular practice of meditation. What an amazing insight for him to connect quitting meditation at least partially to his behavior! Scientists are showing that people who meditate grow bigger brains than those who don't. Researchers at Harvard, Yale and the Massachusetts Institute of Technology found the first evidence that meditation can alter the physical structure of our brains. Brain scans they conducted reveal that experienced meditators boasted increased thickness in parts of the brain that deal with attention and processing sensory input. In Phil Jackson's book *Sacred Hoops*, the author details how he introduced the Bulls to Buddhist meditation practices, so the players could quiet their minds, concentrate on the game and practice non-reactivity in response to on-court violence. The team even developed a playing strategy based on Taoist principles! More than 600 scientific studies verifying the wide-ranging benefits of the Transcendental Meditation technique have been conducted at 250 independent universities and medical schools in

33 countries during the past 40 years. On April 4, 2009, Radio City Music Hall hosted a David Lynch benefit concert to teach meditation to a million children worldwide. Musicians who performed included Paul McCartney (also a vegetarian), Ringo Starr, Eddie Vedder, Cheryl Crow, Ben Harper and others.

Chiropractic care is among the most misunderstood and vilified healing arts in the U. S. Most chiropractic visits are utilized to help people rid themselves of pain, but those who understand it use it to optimize wellness. Jerry Rice is the new spokesperson for the Foundation for Chiropractic Progress and credits the longevity of his career in large part to chiropractic care. He along with Joe Montana, Tiger Woods, Emmitt Smith, Lance Armstrong, John Stockton, Evander Holyfield and David Beckham all utilize chiropractic care for performance. Tiger is quoted as saying, "Being a chiropractic patient has really helped me immensely...lifting weights and seeing a chiropractor on a regular basis has made me a better golfer. I've been going to chiropractors for as long as I can remember. It's as important to my training as practicing my swing." Dan O'Brien is quoted as saying, "I would not have won the gold medal (Decathlon 1996) if it were not for chiropractic. The very simple science behind the potential of chiropractic care is that it optimizes nerve system function. The nerve system controls everything from the immune system to all the major organs, to the very process of cell regeneration itself. What could be more important to one's health and performance?

There are cases and studies showing chiropractic care reversing or diminishing diseases including Parkinson's disease, multiple sclerosis, asthma, infertility, digestive diseases, AIDS and even polio. Correction and treatment of both acute and chronic polio by chiropractic methods have been unusually successful. A national survey by Science Sidelights [published by the National Chiropractic Association] reveals startling results of chiropractic methods in treating polio cases. In 662 acute cases, there was complete recovery in 473 (71.5%). In 889 chronic cases, complete recovery in 257 (28.9%), marked improvement in 454 (51.1%) slight or no improvement in 178 (20%). This is a documented record, which shows the healing potential of this art even for sufferers of polio.

The Internet revolution and the accelerating rate of technology are driving the new wellness paradigm. There is no longer a way to suppress the information necessary for humanity to elevate past basic biological needs and safety needs into needs of love, self-esteem, confidence, self-actualization and self- transcendence. This project will be a genuinely scientific study into the fundamental nature of human potential.

I am confident that the documentary series *Summer Camp* will deliver an authoritative, enlightening, passionate, emotional, humorous message that will resonate with humans all over the planet. We are in desperate need of inspiration and practical methods of empowerment to propel our children into a greater understanding of health from within, and a greater understanding of the infinite Innate Intelligence that connects us and resides within us all.

2. My Favorite Musicians, extended list- (from the letter *Music Makes the World Go Round*):

Other musical artists whose work I have enjoyed include Otis Redding, Sam Cooke, The Jackson Five, James Brown, BB King, Al Green, Aretha Franklin, Etta James, Duke Ellington, Billie Holiday, Luther Vandross, Chuck Berry, Curtis Mayfield, Smokey Robinson, Chaka Kahn, Kool and the Gang, Lionel Ritchie/the Commodores, Diana Ross, The O'Jays, Rick James, Barry White, Alicia Keys, John Legend, Whitney Houston, Donna Summer, The Isley Brothers, The Four Tops, Eryka Badu, Ben E. King, Bob Dylan, The Rolling Stones, The Who, Led Zeppelin, Jimi Hendrix, Queen, Bob Marley, Boz Scaggs, Pink Floyd, The Doors, The Grateful Dead, Nirvana, Van Halen, Eric Clapton/Cream, Roy Orbison, Tom Petty, The Allman Brothers, Fleetwood Mac, Janice Joplin, The Byrds, The Band, Yes, Jefferson Airplane, Chicago, Rush, Kansas, Foreigner, Boston, Blue Oyster Cult, Aerosmith, The Eagles, America, Talking Heads, The Black Keys, The Cure, Blondie, Terrace Trent Darby, The Smithereens, The Verve, Soundgarden, Alice in Chains, Depeche Mode, Metallica, Annie Lenox, The Pet Shop Boys, The Cranberries, The Clash, Midnight Oil, Morrissey, INXS, Stone Temple Pilots, Phil Collins/Genesis, Hall and Oates, John Denver, Stevie Nicks, Steve Winwood, Seals and Crofts, Seal, Cheryl Crow, Shawn Colvin, Natalie Merchant, Peter Gabriel, Norah Jones, Melissa Ethridge, Indigo Girls, Sinead O'Conner, Madonna, Jewel, Tracy Chapman, KD Lang, Chris Isaac, Steve Perry/Journey, Crowded House, Marc Cohn, Christopher Cross, Aimee Mann, Maroon Five, Take Six, Incognito, Paula Cole, Firefall, Los Lobos, Counting Crows, Dave Matthews, The Gypsy Kings, Joan Osborne, Stephen Bishop, Bobby Caldwell, David Gray, Michael Buble, Harry Connick Jr., Bruce Springsteen, Charlie Parker, John Coltrane, Miles Davis, Glenn Miller, Dave Brubeck, Herbie Hancock, Bonnie Raitt, The Ramones, Tito Puente, Ozzy Osbourne, Green Day, Tina Turner, The Bee Gees, The Pretenders,

Gladys Night, The Mommas and the Poppas, Diana Krall, Bobby Darin, Ambrosia, Kenny Logins, Emerson Lake and Palmer, Frankie Valley and the Four Seasons, Johnny Cash, Willie Nelson, Martin Taylor, Django Reinhardt, Stephen Grappelli, Kenny Rogers, Wynton Marsalis, Branford Marsalis, Dizzy Gillespie, Louis Armstrong, Alex Blake, Manhattan Transfer, Groove Armada, Judy Collins, The Lovin' Spoonful, Ravi Shankar, Sly and the Family Stone, Joe Cocker, Country Joe McDonald, Jackson Browne, The Kinks, Little Richard, Woody Guthrie, Chris Thomas King, Chuck Berry, CCR, Alabama, Leonard Skinnard, Elvis Presley, Mary Chapin Carpenter, James Ingram, the Little River Band, and I'm sure I'm leaving out at least a few!

Jana, Ananda, Adam and Naia
Santa Barbara, Calif.
August 2012

About the Author

Dr. Adam Kleinberg was born and raised in New York City. He has practiced chiropractic in six countries on three continents over the last 14 years, and currently resides and practices in Santa Barbara, California.

He is the currently establishing the non-profit organization *The Shine Your Light Foundation* that is dedicated to mentoring and empowering children into a proactive wellness-based lifestyle.

He remains dedicated to creating a legacy of love and compassion for his own children and for children of all ages everywhere.

CPSIA information can be obtained at www.ICGtesting.com
Printed in the USA
BVOW11s1515180714

359477BV00003B/3/P